Law & Ethics in Coaching

Law & Ethics in Coaching

How to Solve *and Avoid* Difficult Problems in Your Practice

Patrick Williams
Sharon K. Anderson

John Wiley & Sons, Inc.

Copyright © 2006 by John Wiley & Sons. All rights reserved.

Published by John Wiley & Sons, Inc., Hoboken, New Jersey.
Published simultaneously in Canada.

For general information on our other products and services please contact our Customer Care Department within the United States at (800) 762-2974, outside the United States at (317) 572-3993 or fax (317) 572-4002.

Wiley also publishes its books in a variety of electronic formats. Some content that appears in print may not be available in electronic books. For more information about Wiley products, visit our web site at www.Wiley.com.

This publication is designed to provide accurate and authoritative information in regard to the subject matter covered. It is sold with the understanding that the publisher is not engaged in rendering professional services. If legal, accounting, medical, psychological or any other expert assistance is required, the services of a competent professional person should be sought.

Designations used by companies to distinguish their products are often claimed as trademarks. In all instances where John Wiley & Sons, Inc. is aware of a claim, the product names appear in initial capital or all capital letters. Readers, however, should contact the appropriate companies for more complete information regarding trademarks and registration.

Library of Congress Cataloging-in-Publication Data:

Law and ethics in coaching : how to solve and avoid difficult problems
in your practice / [edited by] Patrick Williams, Sharon Anderson.
p.   cm.
Includes bibliographical references and index.
ISBN (10) 0471-71614-6 (cloth)
ISBN (13) 978-0471-71614-3 (cloth)
1. Personal coaching—Practice.   2. Executive coaching—Practice.
I. Williams, Patrick, 1950–   II. Anderson, Sharon K.
BF637.P36L39 2006
658.3'12404—dc22   2005010603

Printed in the United States of America

10   9   8   7   6   5   4   3   2   1

Contents

Contents

About the Contributors

Sharon K. Anderson, PhD

Sharon Anderson is well versed in the area of professional ethics. Her writing and research agenda includes issues such as the ethics of multiple relationships and the ethical sensitivity and decision-making of psychologists and other professionals. She has traveled to national and international conferences to present her research findings, and she has published numerous articles and book chapters on the theory and practice of professional ethics in psychotherapy, and legal issues in psychotherapy. She has professional experience as a licensed psychologist, and she has been the chair of the Colorado State University graduate program in counseling and career development. Dr. Anderson has been described by students as "wickedly enthusiastic" about ethics.

Andrew R. Desmond, JD

Andrew Desmond is an Atlanta-based lawyer, researcher, writer, and real estate investor. He has worked for several large publishing companies and has considerable experience as an entrepreneur and investor.

Dolly M. Garlo, RN, JD, PCC

Dolly M. Garlo is an International Coach Federation professional certified coach, graduate of the CoachInc.com accredited coach training program with post-graduate work as a trained retirement coach, and is a licensed strategic marketing design consultant with Y2Marketing. She brings her combined 25-year professional experience in the health-care industry, law, and business to executive/career, life design and business coaching, consulting, and training, as president of Thrive!! Inc. (*www.AllThrive.com*), which she founded in 1997 prior to retiring from the active practice of law with Garlo Ward, P.C. in Austin, Texas, in 2000. Dolly's current work focuses on business owners and professionals in private practice who want to systematically implement major career transition, succession planning, and/or business exit strategies so they can design their preferred retirement options and create a legacy to both live now and leave for future generations.

Charles Hamrick

With 20 years of experience in the management of multinational corporations, and eight years of experience in coaching top executives of major global corporations, he understands the challenges that people face in creating and meeting their goals in global settings. He has managed companies in most Asian countries, Europe, and North America, serving in chief financial officer and managing director roles. Charles creates and delivers programs on coaching for leaders and global leadership for such corporations as GE, GM, and Microsoft. He conducts Asian business briefings for a broad range of government and business organizations, and has worked with members of the U.S. Congress and Senate, including top government leaders.

He is a graduate of the Institute of Life Coach Training and a member of the International Coach Federation, and currently is the director of Asian operations for ILCT.

His professional education includes engineering at undergraduate and graduate levels, psychology at the graduate level, and an MBA. His language abilities include English, Japanese, Chinese, and Korean.

Margaret Krigbaum, MCC, JD

After practicing law for 11 years, Margaret Krigbaum became a full-time coach. Margaret's business and executive practice extends through 11 countries and 15 different professions.

Margaret is a master certified coach with the International Coach Federation and has been vice president of its board of directors, chair of its application review and credentialing committees, and led tracks at the 2000 and 2003 conventions. She is well known world-wide as a speaker through presentations in China, Australia, throughout Europe, and Japan.

William (Bill) H. Lindberg, JD

William Lindberg is an attorney and a coach. He lives in Santa Barbara, California, and Deer Lake, Minnesota. He is a graduate of the University of Minnesota Law School and is president of the Ash Grove Group, a coaching and consulting company. He serves on the faculty at the Hudson Institute of Santa Barbara and is also the executive director of ACTO, the Association of Coach Training Organizations.

G. Kurt Moore, PhD

G. Kurt Moore received his doctoral degree in interdisciplinary studies in 2005. His research interests include adolescence, ethics, narrative therapy, and dynamic systems theory. Dr. Moore is a licensed psychotherapist, teacher, and musician, and currently lives in Colorado.

Marilyn O'Hearne, MSW, PCC

Marilyn's international clients report increased *PEP* (*P*erformance, *E*ffectiveness, and *P*rofitability, and/or *P*eace, *E*nergy, and *P*rosperity). For 30+ years, she has facilitated development through coaching, counseling, training, writing (*Renewing Your Spirit* workbook, etc.), as well as teaching at universities, ILCT, and in Brazil. Marilyn's gentle strength provides a secure foundation while challenging clients to be their best. (*www.marilynoh.com*)

Debra Robinson, PhD

Debra Robinson is a leadership development coach who understands leadership issues from the perspective of a senior executive, internal and external consultant, coach, and educator/trainer. She has participated in many leadership development programs and has been a leader/coach for these programs as well. Certified in a wide array of leadership assessment tools, Debra conducts executive assessments with follow-up coaching for leaders at various levels in organizations.

Effective leadership requires self-management, people management, and organizational savvy. Debra's coaching work focuses on leadership skill development, creating a leadership mind-set, and personal/professional life management.

Debra received BA, MA, and PhD degrees in education and counseling psychology from the University of Illinois and postdoctoral training in organizational development from National Training Laboratories. She received the professional coach certification from the Hudson Institute of Santa Barbara and achieved master certified coach status with the International Coach Federation.

She is vice chancellor for student affairs at the University of Missouri–Rolla, senior consultant with Harshman & Associates in St. Louis, faculty member for the Hudson Institute Coaching Certification program, and principal in the Global Consulting Partnership.

Heather T. Wagoner, PhD

Heather is a master career counselor (MCC) residing in Miami, Florida. Her research interests include career education, international human resources development, life planning, and self-organizing systems as related to therapy and counseling. She holds both the NCC and NCCC under the National Board for Certified Counselors. She is an adjunct professor at St. Thomas University. (*hhtw2004@aol.com*)

Karen Colby Weiner, JD, PhD

Karen Colby Weiner is an experienced psychologist, attorney, educator, and ethicist who currently is focusing her energy on life and business coaching. She is vice-chair of the Michigan Board of Psychology, and has served as president of both the Women Lawyers Association of Michigan and the Michigan Society for Psychoanalytic Psychology.

For many years Dr. Weiner served as chair of the ethics committee of the Michigan Psychological Association, and she is currently on a brief leave of absence from active involvement as a member of the International Coach Federation ethics and standards committee. She is included in both *Who's Who in America* and *Who's Who in the World*.

Patrick Williams, EdD, MCC

One of the early pioneers of coaching, Pat is often called the ambassador of life coaching. Pat has been a licensed psychologist since 1980 and began executive coaching in 1990 with Hewlett Packard, IBM, Kodak, and other companies along the Front Range. He joined Coach U in 1996, closed his therapy practice six months later, and became a full-time coach. Pat was a senior trainer with Coach U from 1997 to 1998 when he started his own coach training school for therapists only, the Institute for Life Coach Training. He has trained over 1,500 helping professionals at the Institute for Life Coach Training and is now opening offices in Korea, Istanbul, Italy, and Australia.

Pat is also department chair of the coaching psychology program at the International University of Professional Studies (www .iups.edu) and has taught graduate coaching classes at Colorado State University and Denver University. He is also dean of the newly expanding UK College of Life Coaching for North America (www.ukclc.net).

Pat has been on the ICF board of directors for the last three years, and co-chaired the regulatory committee as well. He is passionate about the profession of coaching and ensuring it remains a respected profession. He is the co-author of *Therapist as Life Coach: Transforming Your Practice* and *Total Life Coaching: 50+ Life Lessons, Skills, and Techniques to Enhance Your Practice and Your Life.* His new book on the law and ethics of coaching will be out in the fall of 2005.

Ofer Zur, PhD

Ofer Zur is a psychologist, author, and consultant living in Sonoma, California. He is an ethics, private practice, and forensic consultant as well as a psychotherapist in private practice. He has been teaching ethics, boundaries, and dual relationships, private practice, and metaphor of illness classes for over 15 years. Most recently he published the *HIPAA Compliance Kit,* distributed by W. W. Norton, and co-authored *Dual Relationships and Psychotherapy,* published by Springer. He provides CE online via his website at *www.drzur.com.*

Preface

Welcome to the evolving world of coaching, and more specifically the world of legal and ethical issues in coaching. As editors of this book, we believe we have pulled together the best topics and best authors to address the major concerns in each area. This is the first book in the professional and business coaching field to cover legal and ethical issues. Knowing this, we have designed the text to be thought provoking, practical, and enjoyable to read. Our book begins with chapters that introduce the coaching profession, discuss professional ethics, and articulate an ethical choice-making process for coaches. The following chapters address areas of confidentiality, international perspectives, competence, multiple roles, legal matters, and the future of coaching. A question section begins each of these chapters to stimulate your reading of the material to come. Our book is intended for coaches who are just beginning their practice as well as those who may want to review or visit some areas of concern.

We met for coffee at a local café in 2004 and as Sharon was already teaching and writing on ethics in the field of counseling, and she expressed an interest in learning more about coaching, this book was born. With Patrick's involvement in coaching for the last two decades, it was not too difficult to choose the best of the best to write the desired content. We both are extremely pleased with the professionalism and depth of the chapters contained herein. Please let us know how these are helpful to you in your quest for being a highly qualified and ethical coach.

We would like to acknowledge the following people for assisting with this project: Sharon Hamm for her eye for editing, Dr. Mitchell Handelsman for his contributions to Chapter 3, David Bernstein at Wiley and his very helpful staff, and of course all the contributors to this book . . . thanks for your willingness to write your chapters and for such a professional job. It makes this book a valuable resource in the field of coaching.

Patrick Williams and Sharon K. Anderson
October 2005

Law &
Ethics *in*
Coaching

1

The Profession of Coaching

Its Emergence and Intersection with Ethics and Law

Patrick Williams

Introduction

Although coaching is the latest and hottest trend to invade the workplace and the landscape of personal development, it is not really new. Coaching is a derivative of the best thinking in self-improvement since the turn of the twentieth century. The coaching profession found its place in history—and most recently in the business world—when it exploded into the corporate environment in the 1990s. Today, workplace coaching has dozens of specialty fields for every kind of business concern. Among coaching specialties are personal career coaching, transitions and mergers coaching, start-up venture and entrepreneurial coaching, executive leader coaching, team coaching, and what many call life coaching.

We believe that life coaching is the crucible that contains all coaching, since all coaching is best when it is a whole person approach. You might think of life coaching as the *operating system* much like

Windows XP is for a personal computer. It is always there in the background running all other systems. So whether you are an executive coach, a business coach, a leadership coach, relationship coach, parent coach, teen coach, or any other specialist, if you are coaching a living, breathing human being, you are using life coaching.

In addition, coaching exists for every type and size of business, from one-on-one services for the self-employed sole proprietor to large-scale organizational coaching programs within the top Fortune 500 companies. Boeing International even has a coaching department, and IBM has created an initiative to make coaching available to every one of its many thousands of employees, using credentialed coaches certified by the International Coach Federation. Coaching has proven a worthy investment during its short but remarkable history.

> *"Coaching is the latest and most pervasive evolution in the self-improvement industry."*
>
> —CAREER CONFIDENTIAL

The Roots of Coaching

Coaching evolved from three main streams that have flowed together in modern times:

1. The helping professions, such as psychotherapy and counseling.
2. Business consulting and organizational development.
3. Personal development training, such as Erhard Seminars Training (EST), the Landmark Forum, Tony Robbins and Franklin Covey seminars, and others.

One could argue that Socrates is the earliest recorded model of life and business coaching through his process of inquiry. But then he was killed as a result of the disruptiveness that his persistent and challenging questioning caused. It is, however, the many psychological theorists and practitioners from the early 1900s onward who have significantly influenced the development of the business coaching field. For example, the work by William James, father of psychological theory in America, proposed that people often mask or bury their brilliance. The job of coaches is to help clients discover their brilliance by consciously designing their lives and work. In addition to William James, Carl Jung and Alfred Adler have influenced modern-day coaching. Jung believed in a "future orientation," or teleological belief that we can create our futures through visioning and purposeful living. Adler saw individuals as the creators and artists of their lives, and he frequently involved his clients in goal setting, life planning, and inventing their personal futures—all tenets and approaches in today's coaching. In 1951, during the human-potential movement, Carl Rogers wrote his monumental book *Client-Centered Therapy*, which shifted counseling and therapy to a relationship in which the client was assumed to have the ability to change and grow. This shift in perspective was a significant precursor to what today is called coaching.

Abraham Maslow, the father of humanistic and transpersonal psychology, researched, questioned, and observed people who were living with a sense of vitality and purpose, and who were constantly seeking to grow psychologically and achieve more of their human potential. As earlier psychologists did, Maslow spoke of needs and motivations, but with the view that humans are naturally health-seeking creatures who, if obstacles to personal growth are removed, will naturally pursue self-actualization, playfulness, curiosity, and creativity. This perspective is the foundation of coaching today. Maslow's treatise *Toward a Psychology of Being* (1968) set the framework that allowed coaching to emerge explosively in the 1990s as an outgrowth and application of the human-potential movement of the 1960s and 1970s.

Other theorists such as Roberto Assagioli (psychosynthesis), Fritz Perls (Gestalt theory), and Virginia Satir (family therapy), and many of the solution-focused therapists (e.g., Bill O'Hanlon and Steve DeShazer) also created a bridge from a diagnose-and-treat philosophy to a solution-and-future-oriented approach to assisting clients. Most recently, the influence of Martin Seligman and the field of positive psychology offer much research into positive change and its application to the paradigm of personal and business coaching.

The Coaching Advantage in Both Work and Personal Life

The following description of applied coaching illuminates how it is a powerful service for both work and personal life:

> Whether coaching is beneficial at a personal life level, or in the workplace, the value of coaching in helping people reach desired goals cannot be overstated. Bob Nardelli, the CEO of Home Depot, has said, "Without a coach, people will *never* reach their maximum capabilities." This perspective may or may not be true, but the statement is a powerful testimony to the advantage of coaching. Boardrooms across the globe are sitting up and taking notice, especially when the return on the investment of coaching is measurable, and even significant. (McGovern et al., 2001)

Coaching in the workplace can take a variety of forms. A coach can be contracted to provide individual leader or team/group coaching within an organization, while some organizations hire or train their own full-time coaches as permanent employees. There are advantages to both approaches, and which is used depends on the company and the situation. Also, many workplaces are realizing the value of training their leaders and managers to be coaches themselves, so they can employ the successful tenets of coaching in their management and leadership roles. Leaders are learning to be less command and control and more coachlike (Goldsmith, Lyons, & Freas, 2000; the chapters by Kouzes and Posner, and Crane are particularly informative about leaders as coaches). The results of applied coaching in the workplace have been remarkable.

> *"I never cease to be amazed at the power of the coaching process to draw out the skills or talent that was previously hidden within an individual, and which invariably finds a way to solve a problem previously thought unsolvable."*
>
> —JOHN RUSSELL, MANAGING DIRECTOR, HARLEY-DAVIDSON EUROPE LTD.

Organizations are also adopting coaching as a way to turn problems into possibilities. This coaching culture causes a paradigm shift in the workplace. At a typical business you can find employees complaining around the watercooler (or wherever else they gather today!). But where the culture of coaching is present, complaints are often replaced with comments such as "I could sure use some coaching in . . ." or "That sounds like you should call your coach." Although coaching is a burgeoning profession, it can be a powerful culture once adopted in the workplace and fueled by internal sponsorship, training, and encouragement; and organizations can choose to be comprehensively coached at all levels of the workforce.

When coaching skills are taught to managers, they will then assume the role of coach on occasion. However, because they are not assuming the job of professional coach but are just using some coaching techniques, they are not required to follow the ethical principles of the profession of coaching. It is a wise company that teaches its managers not only the skills and tools of coaching, but the ethical guidelines as well.

Coaching Tools and Their Ethical Application

In the modern-day workplace, coaching utilizes theories and practices that have been around quite a while. These tools, an important part of coaching resources, include Group Dynamics, Johari Window, and 360 Feedback assessments that allow clients to recognize blind spots—those Achilles' heels of behavioral tendencies that block effectiveness—and hidden strengths that could be used more effectively. Style assessments or inventories (such as FIRO-B, Myers-Briggs, Peoplemap, Personal Style Indicator, and DISC) help people learn how to relate to others most effectively. (You can read more about the ethical application of assessments in coaching in Chapter 7.)

For example, Daniel Goleman's model of emotional intelligence (EQ) is very popular, especially because it reinforces what everyone always knew but did not want to admit—that relationships within the workplace are important to the overall success of the organization. Businesses improve (and show healthier bottom lines) if their employees are happier and communicate and function as a team that works well together and resolves conflict early (Buckingham & Coffman, 1999).

Clients in individual coaching obtain results from these assessment tools and make discoveries about themselves; working with a coach

Carol came to me for executive coaching to improve her role as vice president of a department in a major international bank. Carol was generally very happy with her work, but she was having difficulty with her team. Specifically, team members often saw her as an aloof tyrant, which was not her intention. Carol sought coaching to learn how to be a better manager. What she learned, however, was that a better manager is really a coach, rather than a supervisor. A good manager brings out the best in team members, ensuring that the team works efficiently and smoothly. Carol had already completed both the Myers-Briggs assessment and 360 Feedback with her staff. I introduced her to Peoplemap (which contains only 14 questions), and she was amazed at the report her answers generated. Carol's profile showed her general tendencies to be Leader-Task, the most common combination for managers. I coached her using the strengths and blind spots of her personality type, which correlated perfectly with what both the Myers-Briggs and 360 Feedback assessments revealed. Carol learned how to communicate more effectively with the other personality types on her team and to appreciate each person's unique contributions, as well as to anticipate potential conflicts. During coaching, Carol also discovered that she needed to delegate more responsibility to her staff, coach her team rather than manage it, and find opportunities to have more fun while maintaining vision for both herself and the team.

Carol realized that an effective team is like a family, and that relationships can sometimes manifest personality conflicts. Learning the concepts of emotional intelligence helped Carol understand that each team member also has emotional needs in the workplace. Carol administered Peoplemap with the members of her team, and she held two follow-up conferences with them to review the results. Everyone felt acknowledged and empowered to work more effectively as a team, and all members appreciated Carol's openness and willingness to change. She became a model for her team as she also became a coach herself.

helps them understand the information derived from the assessments, determine what changes they want to make, and plan the strategy to reach their desired goals. The coach elicits ideas for how clients can change behaviors. A coach does not *tell* the person, but instead helps the client arrive at a strategy for change. Coaching involves motivational interviewing, directed questioning for discovery, intentional listening, appreciative inquiry, empowerment, consistency, and accountability. *Law and Ethics in Coaching* covers the ethical aspects of the coaching relationship, and the case studies included illustrate the concepts throughout (for example, the proper use of assessments, corporate coaching, and personal or life coaching).

Important Distinctions

Coaching borrows from many fields and applies the innovative thinking of their great pioneers. However, it is important to recognize the major distinctions between coaching and other disciplines such as therapy, mentoring, and consulting. Table 1.1 summarizes some of these distinctions in the context of each discipline's focus, the professional–client relationship, the role of emotions, and the fundamental process each discipline follows.

> *"Part therapist, part consultant, part motivational expert, part professional organizer, part friend, part nag—the personal coach seeks to do for your life what a personal trainer does for your body."*
>
> —KIM PALMER, MINNEAPOLIS–ST. PAUL
> STAR TRIBUNE, 1998

With coaching, minimal attention is given to the past; rather, the focus is on developing the person's future. This philosophical shift

Table 1.1 Distinctions between Coaching and Other Disciplines

	Therapy	Mentoring	Consulting	Coaching
Focus of work	Deals mostly with a person's past and trauma, and seeks healing.	Deals mostly with succession training, and seeks to help the one being mentored to do as the mentor does.	Deals mostly with problems, and seeks to provide information (expertise, strategy, structures, methodologies) to solve the problems.	Deals mostly with a client's present, and seeks to guide the client into a more desirable future.
Relationship	Doctor-patient relationship (therapist has the answers).	Older/wiser-younger/less experienced relationship (mentor has the answers).	Expert-person with problem relationship (consultant has the answers).	Co-creative equal partnership (coach helps client discover own answers).
Emotions	Assumes emotions are a symptom of something wrong.	Is limited to emotional response of the mentoring parameters (succession, etc.).	Does not normally address or deal with emotions (informational only).	Assumes emotions are natural, and normalizes them.
Process	The therapist diagnoses, and then provides professional expertise and guidelines to give the client a path to healing.	The mentor allows student to observe mentor's behavior, expertise; answers questions; provides guidance and wisdom for the stated purpose of the mentoring.	The consultant stands back, evaluates a situation, and then tells client the problem and how to fix it.	The coach stands with the client, and helps the client identify the challenges. Then they work together to turn challenges into victories. The client is held accountable to reach his or her desired goals.

has taken root in a generation that rejects the idea of sickness and seeks instead wellness, wholeness, and purposeful living—both personally and professionally. The coaching relationship allows the client to explore blocks to great success and to unlock dreams and desires. The shift from seeing clients as ill or suffering a pathology, toward viewing them as well, whole, and seeking a richer life, is paramount to understanding the work of coaching. Therapy is about uncovering and recovering, while coaching is about discovering.

Ethics in Coaching

To become a recognized profession, coaching must have professional standards, definitions, ethical guidelines, ongoing research, and credentialing. Beginning in the early 1990s, the coaching phenomenon intensified with the creation of several coach training schools and two major professional associations. In 1996, the Professional Coaches & Mentors Association (PCMA) merged with the International Coaching Federation (ICF), and the ICF led the way as the most recognized international association representing the coaching profession. Standards of practice, credentialing, and ethical guidelines were soon established.

In 2004, the ICF's regulatory committee wrote the following self-governance model:

> The standards and structures built by the ICF over the past decade, which support the emergence of coaching as a valued profession, also provide a solid foundation for the self-governance of our profession. In addition, our rigorous adherence as professionals to these standards and practices provides the necessary assurance that the public is protected from potential harm. ICF's self-governance foundation is comprised of and depends upon

each of the following standards and practices, supported by the efforts of the ICF Board, committees, global representatives, credentialed and member coaches.

◆ *Core Competencies* that define the required skill set of a professional coach and establish the foundation for the professional credentialing examination and accreditation for coach training programs.

◆ *A Code of Ethics* to which ICF Members and ICF Credentialed Coaches pledge commitment and accountability to standards of professional conduct.

◆ *Professional Oversight* through an Ethical Conduct Review process for ICF Members and ICF Credentialed Coaches, which allows the public to report concerns and to be confident of objective investigation, follow-up, and disciplinary action.

◆ *Professional Coach Credentialing*, entailing a stringent examination and review process through which coaches must demonstrate their skills, proficiency, and documented experience in application of coaching core competencies. Credentialing includes Continuing Coach Education requirements for periodic renewal of coaching credentials to ensure continued professional growth and development.

◆ *Professional Coach Training Accreditation* by which coach training programs submit to review and continuing oversight to demonstrate their commitment to the highest standards for curricula aligned with defined core competencies, faculty, structure, proficiency, and ethics to support excellence in the training of coaches.

◆ *Ongoing Self-Regulatory Oversight* initiatives to track the needs and concerns of individual and organizational clients on an international basis, and to demonstrate an active commitment to meaningful professional self-governance.[1]

A second major organization is the International Association of Coaches (IAC), which was officially launched on March 11, 2003, as a nonprofit entity in the state of New Mexico. The stated mission of the IAC is to "further the interests of coaching clients worldwide."

Why is this statement critical? Furthering the interests of clients, rather than focusing solely on the coaching industry, prevents a myopic viewpoint. Why is this commitment radical? Simply because it reorients the entire coaching profession.

This mission allows us to stay ahead of and anticipate evolving trends in client needs, help our members better serve clients, evolve coaching as an industry, and elevate the profession. This radical mission statement underscores the belief that a focus on what is best for the client serves the interests of the profession as well.

Additionally, if coaches focus on forwarding the best interests of their clients, the coaches will naturally evolve and innovate, because those interests will inevitably change. An orientation toward the client helps keep the work of coaching agenda-free.

Finally, this mission statement's focus on the client may be a first for *any* professional association (from www.certifiedcoach.org). As both the ICF and the IAC continue to act as major players in bringing high-quality coaching and professional standards to the field, the effects of their distinct efforts over time will be interesting to observe.

In addition to ethical guidelines, professional competencies, and certification, the coaching profession recently witnessed a tremendous surge of interest in academic research and graduate studies. This

---

[1]From *Coaching Professionalism, the ICF, and You*, written by the 2004 Regulatory Committee of the ICF, co-chairs Diane Brennan and Patrick Williams. Copyright, 2005

attention is a critical step in the further evolution of the profession, and such research and training are necessary for developing a field of knowledge, theoretical orientations, and efficacy studies. Research on the effectiveness of and distinctions among skill sets, competencies, and standardization of education and training is tantamount to any profession finding its place of acceptance in the private and corporate culture.

The historical perspective previously delineated reveals that professional coaching emerged from other major professions (e.g., psychology, counseling, consulting). These professions have written codes of ethics and professional standards. In addition, they typically are regulated by state licensing boards (at least in the United States) and other government oversight entities. These government regulations usually determine requirements for training, maintaining a license, and practice laws.

At this time, coaching is not regulated or monitored by a state agency or regulatory board. It is the current belief that the profession should monitor itself. However, some state mental-health regulatory boards think differently, as the following scenario demonstrates.

The Colorado Case and the Threat to Practicing Coaches

In June 2001, the administrator of the Colorado Mental Health Board, Amos Martinez, wrote an opinion piece in the board newsletter entitled "Coaching: Is This Psychotherapy?" In this article, Martinez contends that coaching, especially personal coaching, meets the very broad definition of psychotherapy in the state of Colorado. Because of that interpretation, word began to spread that coaches in Colorado had to register as unlicensed psychotherapists and follow the regulations in the state's Mental Health Act that pertain to those individuals.

Immediately after reading that newsletter, Lloyd Thomas and I, both of us licensed psychologists and practicing coaches, drove to Denver and met with Amos Martinez to discuss the work of professional coaching, the ICF, its standards of ethics, and so on. Although the meeting was cordial, nothing changed in the next several months. The rumor began to spread across the globe that Colorado was going after coaches, and that the profession was in danger of being lumped together with psychotherapy, a distinction most coaches were trying to clarify.

A Colorado Coach and the State Mental Health Board

In 2003, a case against a Colorado coach brought this whole discussion and the legal issue to a head. An ICF master certified coach who lived and worked in Colorado (although all of her clients lived out of the state) was charged with practicing psychotherapy without a license by the Department of Regulatory Agencies in Colorado. Although the charge was dropped as frivolous, Colorado still demanded that the coach register as an unlicensed therapist, which she refused to do. She was forced to close her practice because she could not afford to hire an attorney to pursue the defense of her position.

That case led to a focused effort by the Colorado Coalition of Coaches to pursue changing the law, and the group hired a lobbyist to help with the effort. After 18 months of hard work by the Colorado Coalition, lobbyists, as well as grassroots support and donations by individual coaches, the International Coach Federation, the International Association of Coaches, the Worldwide Association of Business Coaches, and the Association of Coach Training Organizations, the legislature agreed and approved an amendment to the Mental Health Act that exempted coaching from the legislature's oversight. Details of action taken by the ICF's regulatory committee and information gathered in the United States follow. Because coaching is an international profession, the ICF also began conversations about and research on regulatory concerns and issues in other countries, but those concerns and issues have not warranted the same worldwide attention that matters in the United States have. One reason is that the proliferation of government licensing and regulation of various professions are unique to the United States.

All this is not to say that the coaching profession devalues standards and guidelines for professional behavior. In fact, some coaching associations (e.g., the ICF) have worked hard to delineate professional norms through ethics codes. Such standards have been formulated, amended, tested, and applied within many coaching organizations during the field's evolution.

ICF Regulatory History

The ICF Board of Directors chartered a regulatory committee in the summer of 2002 with the goal of researching, monitoring, evaluating, and proactively contributing to government and regulatory bodies in order to educate, articulate, and develop coaching as a self-regulated profession. As a group and via email, the committee researched and discussed the regulatory activity related to coaching within the United States. The committee chair also held discussions with representatives from CoachVille and the IAC. In addition, the group was in dialogue with a key individual within the field of mediation, and with professionals in financial planning and executive management.

During the committee's initial months, the ICF implemented an ethical conduct review process, a solid step in the process of self-regulation. In addition, the ICF provided the opportunity for members to participate in a conference call with the ICF attorney as Colorado coaches encountered mixed messages about the coaching case and regulation in their state.

The 40-page regulatory report published in March 2003 compiles the statutes, interpretations, notes, and articles related to the key states identified in the ICF regulatory committee's purpose and charter. Colorado, Minnesota, Florida, Washington, and California are states in which coaching was rumored to be considered part of the mental-health field and, as such, states that raised concern that coaches might be required to register as unlicensed counselors. It was not the committee's intent to focus only on coaching versus counseling; however, that was the primary area of concern coaches faced in the key states investigated. The regulatory committee expanded to include a liaison group with members appointed by ICF chapter leaders. In early 2004, these individuals continued the review of all U.S. states and Canada. Currently, there are no requirements for coaches to register or be licensed in any state in the United States or in Canada. New mental-health/behavioral-health laws went into effect in New York, Arizona, and Minnesota in 2003 and 2004. The persons responsible for the implementation of these laws have stated that the intent is to tighten up regulation of those performing counseling and therapy services within the respective states. These laws were not intended to, nor should they, include coaches. However, if an individual practices counseling or therapy without meeting the proper state licensing requirements and also engages in coaching, that individual would be in violation of the state requirement as well as the coaching profession's standards.

The Colorado Mental Health Law was up for sunset review in 2004; the law would either stay the same, dissolve, or undergo revision. The Colorado coaches formed the Colorado Coalition of Coaches in late 2003 and began work to propose legislation to revise the statute.[2] In spring 2004, the governor of Colorado signed into law the bill that contains the legislation proposed by the coalition. Specifically, the new clause within Colorado's mental health statutes

---

[2]See www.coloradocoaches.com for more information about the coalition.

states that "The provisions of this article shall not apply to professional coaches who have had coach-specific training and who serve clients exclusively in the capacity of coaches."

More recently, a concern arose in Ohio, where an aspiring coach contacted the state's Mental Health Board to find out whether there were licensure requirements for coaches. I called and spoke with the representative at the Ohio Mental Health board, and he was relieved to learn that the ICF and coaching standards existed. The official seemed satisfied that coaches properly trained would not be infringing on the profession of psychotherapy and expressed gratitude for the information. As stated previously, there are no licensing requirements for coaches at this time. Coaching does not fall within the mental-health/behavioral-health realm. Distinctions between coaching and therapy or counseling are delineated on the ICF website (www.coachfederation.org/eweb/). Additional documents available from the site include:

- "Top Ten Indicators to Refer to a Mental Health Professional"
- "Professional Coaching Language for Greater Public Understanding"
- "Sample Coaching Agreement"

The ICF is committed to maintaining coaching as a distinct profession, and to strengthening coaching's self-governance model. Interested members are welcome to participate as ICF chapter regulatory liaisons. You may send questions or comments via email to regulatory@coachfederation.org.

Law and Ethics in Coaching is intended to increase awareness of legal and ethical issues in coaching, and to provide information specifically for those who are entering the coaching profession, or who are teaching about or offering consultations about coaching. In the pages that follow, as the authors set forth various aspects of ethical and legal issues related to coaching, keep in mind that this is a work in progress. While we can share certain rubrics with other human service professions, the creation of case law, response to ethical complaints, and training in ethics for coaches will be paramount as the profession continues to evolve and create a knowledge base and best-practices mandates in the years to come.

REFERENCES

Buckingham, M., & Coffman, C. (1999). *First, break all the rules: What the world's greatest managers do differently*. New York: Simon & Schuster.

Goldsmith, M., Lyons, L., & Freas, A. (Eds.). (2000). *Coaching for leadership: How the world's greatest coaches help leaders learn*. San Francisco: Jossey Bass.

McGovern, J., Lindemann, M., Vergara, M., Murphy, S., Barker, L., & Warrenfeltz, R. (2001). Maximizing the impact of executive coaching: Behavioral change, organizational outcomes, and return on investment. *The Manchester Review, 6*(1), 3–11.

2

Foundations of Professional Ethics

Karen Colby Weiner

Objective

This chapter explores the history of ethics, first in the context of its philosophical underpinnings, and then through a look at the evolution of codes of ethics. The reader might question the importance of philosophy to ethics. In fact, philosophy and ethics are inextricably linked. First, the foci of ethics and the content of ethics codes are based on philosophy. Therefore, a discussion of philosophy is necessary to understand ethics in depth. Second, ethics and ethics codes are constantly subject to interpretation. Without an awareness of the philosophical thought that underlies ethics, appropriate interpretation is difficult. This review of both the philosophy and the codification of ethics provides a context within which to understand the current ethical principles of coaching, and, in fact, of all professions.

Pre-Chapter Self-Assessment Test

To begin the discussion of professional ethics, consider the following statements and decide whether you believe them to be true or false:

1. As coaches, we must allow clients to discover their own rules about what is good and bad.

    a. True   b. False

2. Whatever permits our clients to have pleasure in their lives is always good.

    a. True   b. False

3. Benefiting others is always a part of what is considered good.

    a. True   b. False

4. People have a natural tendency to be good.

    a. True   b. False

5. Some acts of morality are necessary, regardless of their consequences for others.

    a. True   b. False

6. No single moral code can be binding on all people all of the time.

    a. True   b. False

7. The value of any behavior can always be judged by its consequences.

    a. True   b. False

8. Religion is a necessary component to define good and bad.

    a. True   b. False

9. What is moral can always be discerned by rational thought.

    a. True   b. False

10. Happiness always corresponds to and includes aspects of goodness.

    a. True   b. False

Philosophical History

It is not possible to pinpoint the exact time in which philosophical and ethical debate began. Approximately 38,000 years ago, however, people we now identify as *Homo sapiens* were carrying on active lives. They had control of fire for cooking and warmth, as well as tools, weapons, and ready ways to preserve food. Some individuals hunted, while others fished and collected honey and nuts (Trager, 1979). In other words, these people had formed an organized society. Most likely, early humans had rules—rules related to morality and immorality, good and bad, right and wrong. Such rules only could have been the product of philosophical and ethical debate, and perhaps some of the issues over which they debated we still struggle with today.

The following review begins with a brief summary of the pre-Socratic history of philosophy. Although Socrates is considered the father of Western philosophical thought, it is important to understand that even Socrates was not the first to contemplate the nature of the universe and those who occupy it (Ruggiero, 2004).

Pre–Socratic History

Only a few pre–Socratic philosophers are viewed as significant (Sidgwick, 1931). Among these few is Pythagoras (580–500 BCE), who was thought to have been the founder of an order or brotherhood that advocated the moral precepts of courage, moderation, loyalty, and obedience to law. Pythagoras' moral and religious aims were based on his belief in transmigration of souls, and he advocated that men should live, as much as possible, in the likeness of God.

In contrast, the Sophists, a group of itinerant teachers, postulated that good and evil were more a matter of choice than of nature. Some Sophists even proposed that what is moral is merely a matter of convenience.

Another significant early philosopher is Heracleitus (540–480 BCE), a forerunner of Stoicism. Heracleitus never worked out a complete ethical system but advocated that our world is a scene of battle and strife in which we need uncompromising reverence for the rational, the natural, and the divine.

A third philosopher was Democritus (460–370 BCE). Although Democritus was a contemporary of Socrates, his doctrine is considered pre-Socratic, because it was free from any sign of influence by Socrates. Democritus (considered a precursor of the Epicureans) seems to be the first thinker to expressly declare that delight and good cheer, given some moderation, are the ultimate or highest good.

Socrates and Those Who Followed

Socrates' teachings were the main point of departure for all the great schools of Western ethical thought. Ruggiero (2004) divides his review of the philosophical history of ethics in Western thought into three periods: the classical, the medieval, and the modern. Although he notes that any division is arbitrary, many historians employ this system, and using it will help organize our discussion.

The Classical Period

The classical period of philosophy spans approximately 1,000 years, from about 500 BCE to 500 CE. Greece, then the center of progressive Western thought, was moving from an agrarian monarchy to a commercial industrial democracy. The city-state was coming into existence and, with it, a new moral focus on the duty of the individual as a citizen. Up to that time, with some exceptions, ethics was not seen as an aspect of personal character and social behavior but as the spiritual counterpart of medicine, and its purpose was to minister to the soul as medicine ministered to the body.

Along with the changes in the structure of Greek society, values were changing. Pericles (495–429 BCE), an Athenian statesman and general, complained that "Among educated men everything was in dispute, political sanctions, literary values, moral standards, religious conventions, even the possibility of reaching the truth about anything" (Barton & Barton, 1984, p. 67). The philosophers attempted to create some understanding of moral standards and truth, and bring order to the chaos.

Socrates (469–399 BCE) rejected both the view that nature or tradition should rule conduct and the view that morality was simply a matter of personal choice or convenience. Rather, he elevated a careful examination of beliefs and behavior, and the logic on which they were based, as the way to happiness. Socrates was also an advocate of moderation. Although he considered a life of reasoning paramount, he acknowledged value in sense perception and bodily pleasures.

Interestingly, what we know of Socrates comes to us only through the writings of his student Plato (427–347 BCE). Plato shared Socrates' emphasis that reasoning leads to the happiest and best life. Plato, however, favored the denial of bodily pleasure.[1] He believed that the real world is the world of ideas rather than the world as perceived by our senses. He viewed the concrete reality of the physical world as a

---

[1]As discussed later in this chapter, Plato's beliefs became the model for later religious ethicists.

mere imperfect reflection of the world of abstract ideas, or forms, timeless and unchanging. Within the world of ideas, Plato saw Goodness as the central fact of the universe. Thus, the primary goal of his ethical system was to gain a vision of the Good.

Aristotle (384–322 BCE), Plato's student and a prolific author,[2] disputed his teacher's theory of forms. Plato did not believe that forms can exist apart from concrete objects ("no form without matter, no matter without form") (Ruggiero, 2004, p. 143). Consistently, Aristotle rejected Plato's belief that Good can exist independent of human experience and personality. Rather, he believed that moral principles exist in daily activities and can be discovered by an examination of those activities.

Returning to some of the thinking more consistent with Socrates, Aristotle proposed that one can attain happiness by pursuing a life of reason. Such a life has two goals: the pursuit of truth through reflection and understanding, and the pursuit of virtue through intelligent conduct (Ruggiero, 2004).

Socrates, Plato, and Aristotle represent a philosophical tradition that emphasizes intellect. Following this tradition were the Cynics and the Stoics, whose philosophies stress overcoming feelings and pursuing duty as revealed by reason.[3] Reason, however, did not hold full sway during the classical period. The value of feelings and desires had advocates in the form of the Cyrenaics and Epicureans. These schools of philosophy measure actions not by their degree of reasonableness but by their degree of pleasure. They favor a philosophy of hedonism.

---

[2]Aristotle wrote approximately 400 works on a variety of subjects. His Nichomachean Ethics was the first systematic discourse on ethics in Western civilization.

[3]The Cynics believed that "no speculative research was needed for the discovery and definition of Good and Virtue [but] … man's well-being [was] … in the rational disregard of pleasure" (Sidgwick, 1931, p. 33); the Stoics believed that "what we call passion is a morbid and disorderly condition of the rational soul" (Sidgwick, 1931, p. 73).

The classical period of philosophical debate posed pleasure against duty. As is clear to every coach, this debate is not limited to history. It continues in both philosophical debate and as a factor in the lives of many who seek the assistance of coaches.

The Medieval Period

The medieval period covers the next 1,000 years of Western philosophy (from about 500–1500 CE), a period significantly influenced by Judeo-Christian thought. The religious influence on philosophy and ethics came with the spread of Christianity across Europe. Ethics in the classical period focused on defining the citizen's relation to the state; this emphasis was replaced in the medieval period by the religious believers' obligations to God as explicated in the Bible and interpreted by the church. The classical focus on human reasoning was now being combined with a focus on obedience to the will of God.

Those considered great thinkers of this period, in fact, were men of the church. For example, Saint Augustine (354–430 CE) made Plato's philosophy of the denial of physical pleasures the basis of Christian ethics. Augustine believed that reason leads to temporal well-being, but faith leads to salvation and eternal happiness. Because life on earth was considered only a preparation for the afterlife, real happiness was not attainable on earth. Thus, it was not the natural, earthly side of life that determined ethical behavior and beliefs, but the supernatural, otherworldly side. Augustine believed in the precepts that individuals have fallen from grace by virtue of original sin, but that they retain free will and responsibility for their actions. He considered virtue possible, but to have significance it must be prompted by faith.

Interestingly, Augustine's devotion to Platonic philosophy was so pervasively adopted during the early Middle Ages that Aristotle was nearly forgotten. However, the great medieval philosopher of the church, Saint Thomas Aquinas (1225–1274 CE), rediscovered Aristotle and adapted his philosophy to Christianity to an extent that it transcended Augustine's views and became the accepted philosophical outlook of the later Middle Ages.

Aquinas proposed that ethics had two dimensions: the natural and the theological. Natural ethics was similar to what Aristotle espoused: the development of reason and practice in living a moral life would lead to earthly happiness. Aquinas then added the belief that theological ethics consisted of achieving the virtues of faith, hope, and charity, which, through God's grace, would lead to eternal life with God. Aquinas' greatest contribution was in allowing people to seek secular knowledge without guilt. This aspect of his philosophy permitted a more scientific view of humanity and ethics that foreshadowed the modern period.

The Modern Period

At the beginning of the modern period, during the sixteenth and seventeenth centuries, religion continued to be the central focus of philosophical ethics. However, a great deal of intellectual upheaval was about to take place. The Protestant Reformation challenged the authority of the Catholic Church and had as its message that each person can interpret the Bible for oneself. The rapid spread of the printing press augmented the dissemination and impact of this idea. In addition, the significance of Aquinas' contribution to intellectual exploration turned the attention of philosophy from religious to scientific explanations through the work of scientists such as Copernicus and Galileo.

Thomas Hobbes (1588–1679 CE) was one of the first philosophers to look at ethics from a totally scientific, mechanistic perspective. In fact, he argued that *mechanistic materialism* was central to both physics and ethics. Hobbes proposed that the rule of self-preservation will result in a morality based on self-interest, and so the concepts of right and wrong can exist only in a civilized society. The only way to control one's self-interest is to have a sovereign to whom one can pledge loyalty.

John Locke (1632–1704 CE) took the similar view that pleasure is the standard utilized to reach moral judgment. Under his reasoning, feelings of pleasure or pain cause us to reflect and reach conclusions about justice and goodness, which, in turn, result in the development of moral views. David Hume (1711–1776 CE) proposed an ethical theory that was somewhat consistent with Locke's. Hume considered the standard of moral judgment to be two-sided: the first part is objective, based on consequences; and the second, and dominant, part is subjective, based on feelings of pleasure. In essence, his view was that what is useful and pleasant will be moral. The philosophies of Hobbes, Locke, and Hume are hedonistic; they look to pleasure and self-interest as the measure of good, albeit in a moderate sense.

Two other philosophers, Kant and Mill, contributed significantly during this period. Immanuel Kant (1724–1804 CE) proposed that the basis of moral action is duty. He believed that reason gives rise to a *categorical imperative*, or obligation that binds all rational people. This imperative requires people to act as if their actions are to be obeyed by everyone, and to always treat others (and oneself) as if the treatment is an end in itself, and not a means to an end.

John Stuart Mill (1806–1873 CE) did not create a system of ethics but instead clarified and supported those principles created by his father, James Mill, and his fellow philosopher Jeremy Bentham. The system was called modern utilitarianism. As the title suggests, the central premise of this view is that the goodness or badness of actions is determined by the goodness or badness of their consequences. In contrast to Kant, Mill was a hedonist, because again pleasure and happiness become the standard of moral judgment. Unlike many hedonists of the past, however, Mill distinguished between higher and lower pleasures, with the former preferred.

History of Codes of Ethics

The codification of ethical principles involves ethics as a discipline that falls within philosophy but focuses on human conduct and moral decisions within the context of particular relationships (Remley & Herlihy, 2001). Such relationships generally occur within professions in which individuals are trained to perform personal services to members of the public. In fact, the word *profession* is Latin for "bound by an oath," and codes of ethics have been identified as the "most important distinguishing feature of a profession" (Havard, 1985, p. 8).

The first of these ethical codes, the Code of Hammurabi (developed around 1700 BCE), pertained to the priest-physician (who embodied in one person the roots of theology and medicine), as well as to other professions (e.g., tavern keepers and servants) typical of the times. The code itself prescribed both laws and punishments, and its rules of ethical conduct were chiseled on an 8-foot column (Weiner, 2004; Barton & Barton, 1984). This code contains the first written evidence of society's concern that professions should be controlled and held accountable (Bass et al., 1996). Five hundred years later, approximately 1500 BCE, Moses presented the Ten Commandments, inscribed upon stone tablets, to the Israelites as principles of moral conduct (Barton & Barton, 1984).

The first known example of a profession-generated code of ethics is the Hippocratic oath. Dating from around 400 BCE, the oath is thought to have been part of a rite of induction into a specific Greek medical guild-like community. Hippocrates wrote guidelines for physicians that are still widely quoted and, in fact, still recited as a pledge by physicians graduating from certain medical schools. The Hippocratic oath incorporates obligations of physicians to members of the public and references many ethical issues with which we still deal. These include what treatments might benefit or harm patients, matters of competence and confidentiality, sexual involvement with patients, and respecting laws in general.

Also in the field of medicine (a seminal source of codes that deals with ethical obligations to the public), a Spanish-born Jewish physician named Moses ben Maimon (better known as Maimonides) (1135–1204 CE) created a prayer that emphasizes the special ethical obligations of physicians. These obligations include not thirsting for profit or fame, and to gladly help all people, whether rich or poor, good or bad, enemies or friends. The prayer continues with the need to see in the sufferer a human being (Barton & Barton, 1984).

There are several other examples of early ethics codes. In India around 1 CE, medical students were required to recite a pledge from the ancient *Charaka Samhita* manuscript. The pledge obligated the student to personal sacrifice and commitment to duty. Confidentiality was to be accorded patients, and the student was to refrain from drunkenness. The student was also prohibited from committing a crime or adultery (Barton & Barton, 1984).

Similarly, in sixth-century China, Sun Szu-Miao authored an ethics code entitled *The Thousand Golden Remedies;* in seventeenth-century China, ethical standards were expressed in Chen Shih-kung's *Five Commandments and Ten Requirements*. The consistency of issues addressed in all early medical codes is demonstrated by the fact that these documents encouraged physicians to treat everyone equally, including the poor who could not pay, and to protect confidentiality (Barton & Barton, 1984).

Currently, codes of ethics emanate from one primary source: a profession's recognition that its members have special obligations to the public, which the profession itself wants to address.[4] For example, prior to World War II, psychology was almost exclusively an academic profession, that is, something that was taught but not practiced. As soldiers began to suffer the effects of war, academicians were pressed into applied practice to aid in the military effort. After the war, these new practitioners continued to practice and to provide clinical training to others, thereby changing the face of the profession. Only after psychologists became clinicians was the need for a code of ethics fully recognized.

A second factor from the same period led to heightened awareness of a greater need for ethical guidelines. Ironically, the German doctors who performed experiments on prisoners in Auschwitz claimed they followed the precepts of science to the extent of seeking truth and attempting to solve problems of disease and injury. However, the Nazi atrocities committed on concentration-camp victims in the name of science not only flouted social norms but ignored the most basic ethical maxim, *primum non nocere* ("Above all, do no harm"). This ethical principle is discussed more recently by using equivalent terms such as *beneficence* and *nonmaleficence* (Kitchener, 2000; Beauchamp & Childress, 2001; Bersoff, 1999).

As a result of the Nazi atrocities, the civilized world saw a need to clarify and emphasize what had seemed so obvious before Hitler. Thus, many new codes of ethics were adopted in the late 1940s. These included the *Nuremberg Code of Ethics on Medical Research* (1946), the World Medical Association's *Declaration of Geneva* (1948), and ethics-code amendments by the American Medical Association (1948).

---

[4]Of course, not only humans benefit from codes of ethics. Those persons involved in animal research, for example, can be bound by codes developed by the professions in which they are trained.

Currently in the United States and elsewhere, it is difficult to identify a profession that has not adopted a code of ethics. This coverage includes, of course, a number of coaching codes of ethics adopted by associations that represent both life and business coaches. It has been said that the search for excellence begins with ethics (Solomon, 1997). However, it is important to note that although codes of ethics are undeniably useful, they cannot instill in individuals the power of ethical judgment required to develop a sense of professional responsibility (Weiner, 2004). Thus, having knowledge of philosophy as a science and as a way of understanding behavior, thought, and the nature of the universe strengthens our personal value systems and our worth as coaches.

Conclusion

As we review the history of philosophy, it becomes clear that definitions of what is good and bad, moral and immoral, right and wrong vary and are subject to interpretation. From the classical period of philosophical history, Aristotle's contemplation resulted in a system of beliefs that, despite the passage of thousands of years, can be considered most relevant to current society. In the medieval period, Saint Thomas Aquinas, with the help of Judeo-Christian concepts, was able to open the door for modern philosophy. Perhaps the most striking lesson to be taken from the history of philosophy is that the subject is an ongoing debate, which suggests that philosophers do not see one right philosophy for everyone. As new thinkers come along and changes take place in societies, different cultural systems and philosophical perspectives are considered.

Codes of ethics are no different; they change with the times and with the cultures in which they exist. As we examine coaching codes of ethics, we hope the review will be with a new appreciation for the philosophical opinions and debates that mark their history and the influence of great thinkers and the societal changes that have shaped them. In the coming chapters, you will work with codes of ethics that apply not to an ancient profession such as medicine, but to a relatively new profession: coaching. Nonetheless, you will be able to see the similarity of issues with which all professions struggle. Hopefully, you will also be able to recognize the inextricable relatedness among philosophy, morality, and ethics and the aspiration to do good, and do right, by our clients.

Case Study

Two individuals contact you and wish to hire you as their coach. You have a lot of experience, but you also have some concerns about taking on each of these individuals. They describe themselves as follows:

- Helena is a young married woman with two children. She wants help in establishing priorities. She hopes to make returning to work her main goal because she wants more excitement in her life. Helena double-checked the confidentiality of the sessions and, once reassured, admitted that the only excitement she currently has is an affair she is engaging in with a neighbor. She meets the neighbor when her children are at school. She expresses no remorse, only gratitude that one part of her life is so fulfilling.

- Martin is a married man in his forties. He has suffered for about five years from an inability to make decisions. He wants to work with you on spiritual issues, and on his constant concerns about the ramifications of his decisions. Martin is so concerned about doing the right thing that at times he feels frozen. He explains that since he became a born-again Christian, he has become more aware of his behavior and is consumed by worry that he might do the wrong thing. He feels he cannot predict how things will turn out, so he even worries that his well-intended actions could have negative consequences. He has prayed about this, but his prayers have not resolved his uncertainty. His fondest wish is that he could feel free to just make a decision based on what feels right.

Questions

1. Helena's outlook on life is hedonistic; assuming this perspective is inconsistent with your philosophy, could you work with her?
2. If you chose to work with Helena, how would you handle the agenda for the coaching? Would you allow her to set the agenda (returning to work is the first goal), or would you require that issues related to morality be addressed first?
3. Do you think it is possible that coaching Helena on her own goals would lead at some point to a questioning of Helena's values and changing Helena's thinking about what is right and wrong?
4. Do you think that coaching Martin could help him resolve his indecisiveness without bringing into question his religious views?
5. If you coach Martin, what direction would you take? For example, could you help him by questioning what he believes God wants of him?
6. Do you believe that only a Christian coach should work with Martin? Could someone with other philosophical or religious beliefs understand how to help him?
7. Do you believe that coaching would undermine Martin's faith in any way?
8. Describe the type of philosophy (not religion) that you believe a coach should have to be a good coach for Martin.

REFERENCES

Barton, W., & Barton, G. (1984). *Ethics and law in mental health administration.* New York: International Universities Press.

Beauchamp, T., & Childress, J. (2001). *Principles of biomedical ethics* (5th ed.). Oxford: Oxford University Press.

Bersoff, D. (1999). *Ethical conflicts in psychology* (2nd ed.). Washington, D.C.: American Psychological Association.

DeMers, S., Ogloff, J., Peterson, C., Pettifor, J., Reaves, R., Retfalvi, T., Simon, N., Sinclair, C., Tipton, R., & Bass, L. (1996). *Professional conduct and discipline in psychology.* Washington, D.C.: American Psychological Association.

Havard, J. (1985). Medical confidence. *Journal of Medical Ethics 11*(1), 8–11.

Kitchener, K.S. (1999). *Foundations of ethical practice, research, and teaching in psychology.* Mahwah, New Jersey: Lawrence Erlbaum Associates.

Remley, T., & Herlihy, B. (2000). *Ethical, legal, and professional issues in counseling.* Upper Saddle River, New Jersey: Prentice Hall.

Ruggiero, V. (2004). *Thinking critically about ethical issues* (6th ed.). Boston: McGraw-Hill.

Sidgwick, H. (1931). *Outlines of the history of ethics for English readers* (6th ed.). Boston: Beacon Press.

Solomon, R. (1997). *It's good business: Ethics and free enterprise for the new millennium.* Lanham, Maryland: Rowman & Littlefield.

Trager, J. (Ed.) (1979). *The people's chronology: A year-by-year record of human events from prehistory to the present.* New York: Holt, Rinehart, and Winston.

Weiner, K. (2004). *The little book of ethics for coaches: Ethics, risk management, and professional issues.* Bloomington, Indiana: AuthorHouse.

3

Ethical Choice

An Outcome of Being, Becoming, and Doing

Sharon K. Anderson, Heather T. Wagoner, and G. Kurt Moore

Objective

Imperative to the repertoire of all professional coaches is an awareness of and focus on the ethical dimensions and responsibilities of their role. Unfortunately, many individuals are unprepared, for various reasons, to deal with these issues as they arise. In ethical terms, this lack of preparedness and awareness can present problematic consequences that are not in the best interest of the client, the coach, or the coaching profession. To use best judgment and appropriate conduct with their clients, professional coaches need to realize that they will draw upon several factors (either consciously or unconsciously): their development as ethical and virtuous persons, their professional ethical identity, and their understanding and commitment to professional ethics (Handelsman, Gottlieb, & Knapp, 2005, p. 59).

Just as coaches have a responsibility to encourage clients' self-discovery and hold clients accountable for their own lives and work, this chapter encourages a parallel process for coaches in their role as ethical agents (ICF, 2005). Several factors contribute to professionals as they choose an ethical course of action in their work; this chapter explores these factors and defines various concepts related to making ethical choices.

Introduction

As professionals, we make choices every day. Some of these choices are about who, and how, we will serve. Our choices about best practice go beyond the minimum of what is expected or called for. Possibly the most difficult choices are those in the arena of moral or ethical dilemmas. The phrase "damned if I do, damned if I don't" characterizes the drama of ethical dilemmas, which are problems with ethical dimensions whose options for resolution feel uncomfortable and complex. Kitchener (2000) defines an ethical dilemma as "a problem for which no choice seems completely satisfactory, since there are good but contradictory reasons to take conflicting and incompatible courses of action" (p. 2). Kidder (1996) defines an ethical dilemma not as a choice between right and wrong, but as a choice between two rights. Resnick (1997) notes that an ethical dilemma is a situation in which a person can choose between at least two different courses of action that, from an ethical point of view, appear to be equally justified (or unjustified).

No matter what the choice at hand may be, whether it comprises an ethical dilemma or simply a decision about how to accomplish best practice, we draw upon parts of ourselves and factors that have contributed to our development to take action or make a choice.

Contributing Factors to Ethical Choices

A review of the literature might lead one to think that ethical decision making in coaching represents a cognitive process that is isolated to a single moment in time when a coach faces a particular dilemma or best-practice issue. We propose instead that several factors contribute to being able to choose an ethical course of action. These factors include the individual's personal character, ethics training, and moral reasoning, and in addition to these, a professional ethical identity, developed through adapting or acculturating to the coaching profession.

Personal Character and Ethics

First, *personal character* refers to what people bring with them in terms of their morals and ideals about right and wrong when entering the professional realm. Kitchener articulates it this way: "Individuals have ethical beliefs and emotional responses to problems, which result from what they have learned about what they ought and ought not to do from their parents, teachers, and society" (2000, p. 12). To elaborate, Handelsman, Gottlieb, and Knapp observe that "Students enter training with their own moral value traditions and concepts but are confronted with new ethical principles and rules, some of which may be inconsistent with their ethics of origin" (2005, p. 59). Some coaching training programs might overlook this aspect of the individual's character, yet it is an important facet in the development of professionals. Consciously or unconsciously, this prior learning and ethical belief system impacts ethical choices in the professional realm.

Moral or Ethical Reasoning Capability

A subset of the character, or personal ethics, component is one's capability for moral or ethical reasoning. Moral reasoning as a process involves evaluating a particular event, action, and consequence in the context of a standard: cultural, religious, or ideological. According to Rest (1979), moral reasoning is one's conceptual and analytical ability to frame sociomoral problems, using one's standards and values, in order to judge the proper course of action. A simpler definition, according to Resnick, is that moral reasoning is the process in which one deliberates about a moral or ethical choice—"a moral or ethical choice is a situation where a person can make a decision that involves some ethical or moral principle or concept" (1997).

Virtue Ethics and Character

A professional who goes beyond what is expected—beyond what is written in the professional ethics code or rules—is an exemplar and a consummate professional. That professional is drawing upon some aspect of character—a virtuous character—to exceed external ethical codes, rules, and expectations.

Kitchener (2000) uses the term *virtue ethics* to indicate what those professionals with good character, in this case coaches, use to assess and comprehend ethical or moral dilemmas more accurately, and, as a result, make better decisions. Only in recent years has professional literature (especially that of the helping professions) been discussing the relationship between personal character and virtue ethics (Jorden & Meara, 1990; Meara, Schmidt, & Day, 1996). Meara et al. argue that virtue ethics attends to an individual's motivation, emotion, character, and ideals. Virtue ethics asks the question, "Who or what kind of person should I be?" (Meara et al., 1996; Pence, 1991). Some might argue that trying to teach someone of poor moral character to be ethical is like planting a seed in poor or contaminated soil, hoping for a healthy plant when in fact the plant is unlikely to thrive and may even become deformed (Brown, 1994; Kitchener, 2000). This line of thought contends that this kind of individual, even after training, will probably develop a "deformed sense of ethical responsibility" (Kitchener, 2000, p. 43). Some suggest that a person of good character, or someone with virtuous moral character, is more likely to demonstrate greater understanding of the moral or ethical issue and then be more likely to choose the moral ideal or make an ethical choice (Kitchener, 2000, pp. 43–45).

According to Kitchener (2000), discussions about virtue ethics does not support that a person is "born with either a virtuous or a vicious moral character" (p. 45). In all actuality, these virtuous qualities "develop over time with practice, modeling, feedback, and teaching" (Kitchener, 2000, p. 45; see also Annas, 1993; Gert, 1988; MacIntyre, 1981).

Virtues Essential for Coaching

A question one might ask is, "What kind of character is vital for being a good coach?" Ethics literature in various disciplines suggests that there are several different virtues necessary for a professional to effectively work with or offer services to people. In the area of medical practice, Beauchamp and Childress (1994) have discussed the virtues of integrity, compassion, discernment, and trustworthiness. In psychology, Meara et al. (1996) highlight respectfulness, integrity, prudence, and benevolence as part of moral character. Kitchener (2000) adds to this list by including the traits of trustworthiness and compassion. Velasquez, Andre, Shanks, and Meyer (2005) include integrity, honesty, self-control, courage, compassion, and generosity in business ethics.

To answer the question posed previously, we provide the following list of virtues that coaches need to draw upon:

◆ *Prudence or practical wisdom*—the ability to critically think through moral or ethical issues and apply insight in a manner that works for the best interest of the client (Kitchener, 2000)

- *Integrity*—"a consistent commitment to do what is best," even in difficult situations (Halfon, 1989, p. 8)

- *Trustworthiness*—a way of being that demonstrates dependability, credibility, and honesty (Beauchamp & Childress, 1994; Kitchener, 2000)

- *Respectfulness*—an attitude that shows consideration for another, especially when one's actions will have some impact upon the other (Darwell, 1992)

- *Compassion*—a profound disquiet and heartfelt care for another's situation and well-being (Beauchamp & Childress, 1994)

Drawing upon these virtues will result in sensitivity to the issues or decisions at hand, and a propensity to choose in the client's best interest.

Professional Culture and the Process of Acculturation

Every profession has a culture. The world of coaching is no different, and the adaptation to the coaching culture is another key contributing factor to choosing ethical practice. Components that comprise a professional culture include many factors, such as the following:

- The leaders and their philosophical views of the profession and what it means to be professional

- The common language of the profession

- Written and unwritten codes of ethics

- Training available within the profession

- The profession's values

- Traditions within the profession

- The profession's history
- The collective influence of all the members of the profession

When a person joins the world of coaching, he might assume that being effective and making ethical choices mean obtaining some training and learning about the ethical code of conduct for coaches. However, ethical behavior involves a more comprehensive journey. Handelsman, Gottlieb, and Knapp (2005) state that

> Becoming an ethical professional is more complex than simply following a set of rules or doing what one sees one's mentors do . . . [It] involves more than teaching certain professional rules to morally upright people who will easily understand and implement them. (p. 59)

Becoming part of the coaching culture is not automatic. It involves an adapting or acculturating process. Handelsman, Gottlieb, and Knapp (2005) contend that the ethical culture of a profession (in this case, coaching) might be quite different from a person's ethics of origin or one's personal ethics. For example, some new coaches or coaches in training might find it counterintuitive to not lead, give direction, or advise in the coaching relationship with their clients. In their personal lives, they know that friends have sought them out for their sage wisdom and they thought this would be part of coaching. But as coaches learn, giving advice takes away from clients' autonomy and power of choice.

Berry and Sam define acculturation as "a set of internal psychological outcomes, including a clear sense of personal and cultural identity, good mental health, and the achievement of personal satisfaction in the new cultural context" (1997, p. 299). Handelsman, Gottlieb, and Knapp (2005) suggest that this definition of acculturation can be applied to the idea of one's professional ethical identity. They use the phrase *ethical acculturation* to suggest that *ethical* can be substituted for *cultural* in the previous definition, to read as follows: ethical acculturation is "a set of internal psychological outcomes, including a clear sense of personal and [ethical] identity, good mental health, and the achievement of personal satisfaction in the new [ethical] context." The more the individual can adapt to the new culture—in this case, the coaching culture, with its values, philosophy, and traditions— while retaining aspects of one's ethics of origin or personal ethics, the better the fit, and the more likely the individual is to have a coherent professional ethical identity and, possibly, to demonstrate what Gardner, Csikszentmihalyi, and Damon (2001) call *good work*. In this sense, the individual draws upon the coaching culture's training and professional ethics, as well as her own ethical sense, to deliver best practice and resolve ethical dilemmas.

Those professionals who struggle to make sense of the coaching culture's values and ethics in light of their own personal values and ethics might be more susceptible to ethical problems (Handelsman, Gottlieb, & Knapp, 2005, p. 61). Such vulnerability might become evident in behaviors such as failing to recognize their limits in competency, deciding to compromise ethical standards when faced with pressure, or opting out of professional affiliations with coaching associations because they see little value in accountability and ethical codes. (For a more in-depth explanation about adaptation to a new culture and the development of a professional ethical identity, see Berry & Sam, 1997, and Handelsman, Gottlieb, & Knapp, 2005.)

Ethical Decision–Making Models

Tarvydas, Cottone, and Claus (2003) provide a review of several ethical decision-making models. They present an analysis of these models based upon whether the models are theoretically or philosophically based or practice based. In reviewing these models, one might conclude that the ethical decision-making process is rather cognitive, possibly linear, occurring at a moment in time, detached from the personal character of the professional and disconnected from the client who is receiving services, and separate from the coaches' views of themselves as professionals. As previously stated, ethical choices (either in the face of a dilemma or when going beyond the expected) occur because of more than proper ethics training. To explain our proposed model, we provide a brief overview of three approaches that contribute to our understanding of the ethical-choice process. We chose *ethical-choice process* to describe our approach rather than *ethical decision-making model* because the word *choice* articulates a more active, and encompassing, process of realization and then carrying out the decision made. For example, it is possible that a coach might decide to be clear about his limits of competence, but in practice does not refer a client who needs someone else's expertise because of the coach's own financial desires. Also, the word *process* indicates the fluid and nonlinear nature of the model. Each aspect of the process can influence another. Therefore, a choice may take a different shape than originally thought because of new information or insights.

Kitchener's Model

In 1984, Kitchener presented a seminal work on ethical decision making in psychology. She offered this model as a way for one to view or process through ethical dilemmas in order to check intuition or gut-level responses and enter into a more reflective, critical analysis of the issue at hand; or when ethical codes or guidelines are inadequate or provide conflicting advice. Kitchener's model brings together Hare's discussion (1981) of levels of moral reasoning (intuitive and critical-evaluative) and the ethical principles of nonmaleficence, beneficence, autonomy, and justice presented by Beauchamp and Childress (1979) in biomedical ethics, to which Kitchener added the ethical principle of fidelity.

Rest's Model

In the early 1980s, James Rest proposed a theory of moral behavior (1983). Rest suggested that moral behavior was more than just a cognitive process. He expanded Kohlberg's moral development theory (1969, 1980) to include several other components that are necessary for moral behavior to occur. More specifically, in 1994, Rest defined four components as "the major determinants of moral behavior" (pp. 22, 23–24). He identified them as follows:

- *Moral sensitivity*—to interpret a situation as an ethical one, meaning that one's choice or decision will affect the welfare (positively or negatively) of another
- *Moral decision making*—to think through or evaluate alternative courses of action based on ethical or moral reasoning and to identify the best or ethically ideal solution
- *Moral motivation*—to identify and decide between conflicts of interest such as personal gain or gratification or the good of the client; to decide whether to fulfill one's moral or ethical ideal
- *Moral character*—to put in place, through "ego strength, perseverance, backbone, toughness, strength of conviction, and courage," the moral or ethical ideal

Rest summarizes that:

Moral failure can occur because of deficiency in any component. All four components are determinants of moral action. In fact, there are complex interactions among the four components, and it is not supposed that the four represent a temporal order such that a person performs one, then two, then three, then four—rather, the four components comprise a logical analysis of what it takes to behave morally. (1994, p. 24)

Tarvydas' Model

Tarvydas' model for ethical behavior, introduced in 1997, draws upon the previous models (Kitchener and Rest). It incorporates principle and virtue ethics while reminding the decision maker of the contextual considerations that foster sensitivity to differences in multicultural and diverse milieus and communications. In addition, her model encourages the professional to maintain a "stance of reflection" throughout the decision-making process (Tarvydas, Cottone, & Claus, 2003, p. 90).

Our Model: Ethical Choice—An Outcome of Being, Becoming, and Doing

Remembering that ethical choice is the result or outcome of several factors, we've used a funnel shaped figure as our visual representation of this process (see Figure 3.1). As previously stated, we suggest that when a professional is confronted by an ethical situation or dilemma, her recognition and experience of that situation is influenced by several factors. The process is impacted by and encompasses the character of the individual, her propensity toward virtue ethics, professional ethical identity, and ethics training. Then, on a more conscious level, she moves to the bottom circle, "Components of Ethical Behavior". This bottom circle is a key piece to the choice process and, as a result, we have identified some questions that a coach might ask herself to tap into her cognitions, motivations and emotions and that facilitate a collaborative relationship between the client and herself.

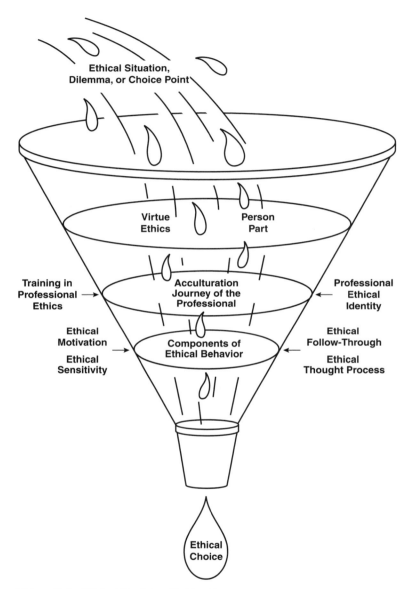

Figure 3.1   Ethical Decision-Making Process

Component 1—Ethical Sensitivity. These questions speak to coaches' awareness that their choices affect others positively and negatively:

- *What strikes you?* In other words, awareness is everything; in counseling terms, being present in the moment, and projecting the consequences of behavior.

- *What calls to your attention?* As a coach, your obligation to the client involves careful attention to details—both those that are stated and those that are unstated.

- *Who is involved in this situation?* In simple terms, who are the key individuals and their context, both as known by you, the coach, and by the client?

- *What makes you think, "Uh-oh, this doesn't feel right"?* This response is often described as a gut, intuitive feeling that something is awry.

- *What makes you think, "Yes, this feels good or right"?* How do you know that what you are doing is effective, or has efficacy? What is good or right for one client might be very different for another. How will you know this?

- *What are the issues related to diversity? To differences between my client and me? To oppression or discrimination?* Awareness of diversity is not enough. As a practitioner, you must be cognizant of your worldview and that of your client.

- *How does my point of privilege affect my sensitivity to this issue?* As an individual of privilege, you as coach must be able to look outside yourself at the potentialities and constrictions that a client might have experienced. Moving from your subjective experience to an objective realism can assist you in seeing privilege's impact (Anderson & Middleton, 2005).

Component 2—Ethical Thought Process. These questions highlight Kitchener's decision-making model (2000):

- *What do I know about the situation?* When you are assessing a situation, this question allows you to see what exists and what might not be readily visible.

- *What else do I need to know?* In Kitchener's model of upholding the dignity of the individual, to have a full sense of an ethical dilemma is necessary.

- *What does the ethical code say?* The ethical code provides a guideline of imperatives that regulate and clarify your behavior as coach and your relationship with the client.

- *What are the legal issues?* The legal issues provide a minimum of expectations to consider within your professional realm as coach. Legal issues offer a precedent from which to minimally consider the outcome of a situation.

- *With whom should I consult?* As a coach, you need to understand the options available in terms of the professional bodies, authorities, and resources that can provide guidance when problematic ethical dilemmas arise.

- *What does the client think is ethically appropriate?* Inherent in the client's rights is her consideration of a situation. Ultimately, if one considers Kitchener's work, loyalty to the client is central.

- *If I were the client, what would I hope my coach would do?* Asking this question offers an opportunity for you as coach to parallel process the issue at hand and step outside the role of practitioner to consider the client's perspectives and wishes.

Component 3—Ethical Motivation and Competing Values. These questions search out the heart of the matter, the values conflicts within the coach:

- *What are the conflicts inside me?* This question presumes a level of introspection on your part, as coach.

- *Who benefits from which course of action?* As coach, you must question the courses of action in detail, hypothetically seeing the potential results of any chosen action or behavior.

- *What core values (personal and professional) are being stretched?* As coach, you must be centered in your personal and professional development to understand your own limitations.

- *What core values (personal and professional) are being strengthened?* As coach, you must also have some metacognitive process to observe yourself thinking or reflecting on actions that relate to your core personal and professional values, and how you allow yourself to grow as an individual.

- *How does my client win or lose, depending on the course of action?* You as coach with your client must identify what fosters the client to gain clarity or win in a situation, and what impedes progress or causes the client to lose ground. Actions have consequences—seemingly benign actions might be good for one client and yet hinder another.

- *With whom do I need to consult to see the conflicts as clearly as possible?* Again, as coach, you must know and use your professional resources. You should never operate in isolation in your coaching role.

Component 4—Ethical Follow-Through. These questions prompt implementation of the choice:

- *To whom do I want to be accountable?* As coach, you must understand the maximum extent of your accountability as outlined, for example, in the ICF's ethical codes and the laws that regulate your coaching practice.

- *Who are people from whom I can get encouragement?* As a professional coach, you must be connected integrally with those other professionals in your domain.

- *What core values do I need to draw upon?* Knowing and identifying basic core values is essential to provide you with a compass, especially in issues of conflicting loyalties.

- *What do I need to let the client know?* The client has rights in many respects and must know about potential issues of concern. For example, if as coach you provide a test to assess the client, your client has a right not to be tested, and to give informed consent to be tested.

It is important to recall that Rest (1994) did not see these components as sequential in nature, meaning that component 1 happens first, then component 2, and so on. He did, however, state, "Each of these processes must have occurred for moral behavior to have occurred" (p. 19).

Case Study

Select one or more of the following scenarios, and for each consider the questions we have proposed in the four components. Assess how your process, and choice, are being influenced by your beliefs, values, and character, your professional ethical identity determined by your acculturation into the coaching culture, and your knowledge of professional ethics.

1. During the course of a coaching relationship, you and a client find that you very much enjoy each other's company and are physically attracted to each other.
2. A business hires you to coach some of its managers during a challenging transition. As part of the agreement, the HR department insists that its director have full access to all of your session notes.
3. During a coaching session, you discover information about a client that could create financial problems for the company he works for—the company that is paying you to coach him.
4. An HR employee tells you that one of your clients is being considered for termination due to corporate downsizing, but asks you not to tell your client yet.
5. You are contracted to coach several executives at a corporate office. One of them describes her personal hatred for another executive in the group and details her plans to sabotage his career.
6. A client tells you about a new product that his company is about to unveil, and he advises you to buy its stock quickly.
7. A large company offers to pay you to perform all coaching work for it—a very lucrative contract. However, your current girlfriend works there; she not only is a potential client but also could benefit from any information you share with her.

Conclusion

Ethical decisions and ethical practice in coaching are paramount to good work. This chapter presents a discussion and model that suggest a coach's process in decision making is not isolated to a moment in time, or to a specific situation. The process is impacted by several other factors: the coach's character, development of virtue ethics, training in ethics, and professional ethical identity, which develops through acculturation to the coaching profession. Lastly, the coach goes through a more conscious process to arrive at an ethical choice.

REFERENCES

Anderson, S.K., & Middleton, V.A. (Eds.). (2005). Explorations in privilege, oppression, and diversity. Belmont, CA: Thomson Brooks/Cole.

Annas, J. (1993). *The morality of happiness.* Oxford: Oxford University Press.

Beauchamp, T.L., & Childress, J.F. (1979). *Principles of biomedical ethics* (1st ed.). Oxford: Oxford University Press.

——— (1994). *Principles of biomedical ethics* (4th ed.). Oxford: Oxford University Press.

Berry, J.W., & Sam, D.L. (1997). Acculturation and adaptation. In J.W. Berry, M.H. Segall, & C. Kagitcibasi (Eds.), *Handbook of cross-cultural psychology,* Vol. 3: Social behaviour and applications (2nd ed.) (pp. 291–326). Boston: Allyn & Bacon.

Brown, L.S. (1994). *Subversive dialogues: Theory in feminist therapy.* New York: Basic Books.

Darwell, S.L. (1992). Two kinds of respect. In J. Deigh (Ed.), *Ethics and personality: Essays in moral psychology* (pp.65–78). Chicago: University of Chicago Press.

Gardner, H., Csikszentmihalyi, M., & Damon, W. (2001). *Good work: When excellence and ethics meet.* New York: Basic Books.

Gert, B. (1988). *Morality: A new justification of the moral rules.* New York: Oxford University Press.

Halfon, M.S. (1989). *Integrity: A philosophical inquiry.* Philadelphia: Temple University Press.

Handelsman, M.M., Gottlieb, M.C., & Knapp, S. (2005). Training ethical psychologists: An acculturation model. *Professional Psychology: Research and Practice 36,* 59–65.

Hare, R. (1981). The philosophical basis of psychiatric ethics. In S. Bloch & P. Chodoff (Eds.), *Psychiatric Ethics* (pp. 31–45). Oxford: Oxford University Press.

International Coach Federation (ICF) (2005). The International Coach Federation Code of Ethics. Retrieved September 12, 2005, from *http://www.coachfederation.org/eweb/.*

Jorden, A.E., & Meara, N.M. (1990). Ethics and the professional practice of psychologists. *Professional Psychology: Research and Practice 21,* 107–114.

Kidder, R. (1996). *How good people make tough choices.* New York: Fireside.

Kitchener, K.S. (1984). Intuition, critical evaluation and ethical principles: The foundation for ethical decisions in counseling psychology. *Counseling Psychologist, 12,* 43–55.

———— (2000). *Foundations of ethical practice, research, and teaching in psychology.* Mahwah, New Jersey: Lawrence Erlbaum.

Kohlberg, L. (1969). Stage and sequence: The cognitive-developmental approach to socialization. In D. Goslin (Ed.), *Handbook of socialization theory and research* (pp. 347–480). Chicago: Rand McNally.

———— (1980). High school democracy and education for a just society. In R.L. Mosher (Ed.), *Moral education: A first generation in theory and development* (pp. 20–57). New York: Praeger.

MacIntyre, A. (1981). *After virtue.* Notre Dame, IN: University of Notre Dame Press.

Meara, N.M., Schmidt, L.D., & Day, J.D. (1996). Principles and virtues: A foundation for ethical decisions, policies and character. *Counseling Psychologist, 24,* 4–77.

Pence, G. (1991). Virtue theory. In P. Singer (Ed.), *A companion to ethics* (pp. 249–258). Oxford: Blackwell.

Resnick, D. (1997). Some definitions of key ethical concepts. Retrieved September 20, 2004 from http://www.scicom.lth.se/fmet/ethics_03.html.

Rest, J.R. (1979). *Development in judging moral issues.* Minneapolis: University of Minnesota Press.

———— (1983). Morality. In J. Flavell & E. Markman (Eds.), *Handbook of child psychology: Vol. 3, Cognitive development* (pp. 556–629). New York: Wiley.

———— (1994) Background: Theory and research. In J.R. Rest & D. Narvaez (Eds.), *Moral development in the professions: Psychology and applied ethics.* Hillsdale, NJ: Lawrence Erlbaum.

Tarvydas, V.M., Cottone, R.R., & Claus, R.E. (2003). Ethical decision-making processes. In R.R. Cottone & V.M. Tarvydas (Eds.), *Ethical and professional issues in counseling* (2nd ed.). Columbus, OH: Merrill/Prentice Hall.

Velasquez, M., Andre, C., Shanks, T., & Meyer, M.J. (2005, April 8) Ethics and virtue. Retrieved September 12, 2005, from Markkula Center for Applied Ethics, Santa Clara University, CA, http://www.scu.edu/ethics/practicing/decision/ethicsandvirtue.html.

4

Competence

Getting, Growing, and Measuring Coaching Ability

Margaret Krigbaum

"When love and skill work together, expect a masterpiece."

—JOHN RUSKIN

Objective

Every coach wants to be a master at coaching. Every client wants a masterful coach. The question both ask is, "How do I know?" More specifically, the coach asks, "How do I know that what I am doing is masterful?" and the client asks, "How do I know that what I am getting is masterful?" Coaches want to gauge whether their coaching is both good and valuable to the client. Clients want to know how to find a good coach and then be able to tell that the coaching is valuable to them. This chapter is meant to help the coach and the client understand and measure coaching competence. By the end of this chapter, both will know how coaches develop and grow competence.

In addition, both will know how to measure the success of a coaching relationship.

Competence, as this chapter discusses it, is a scale of growth for the coach. A good coach acquires an initial level of competence and uses it well. A masterful coach sees that initial level of competence as a foundation for continual learning and development. Thus, the measure of competence is an ever-enlarging conversation where the coach continues to inquire about her level of skill and the best ways to improve that level of skill. This chapter discusses how coaches gain and assess initial competence, how coaches cultivate additional competence, and how both the coach and client can quantify competence together. In order to start the inquiry, it is first necessary to understand what coaching competence is.

Defining Competence

A competent coach possesses a skill set that is distinct. That skill set has been defined by professional bodies in the coaching profession. In particular, the International Coach Federation (ICF) has created not only a definition of coaching, but also a set of 11 competencies and 69 supporting skills that define how a coach should interact with clients.[1]

The competencies require that the coach has a connected relationship with the client, a base level of trust and intimacy in that relationship, an awareness of who the client is and what the client wants, and an ability to listen on several levels. The coach should approach the client from a place of curiosity rather than as an expert in subject

---

[1]The ICF is the oldest, independent, nonprofit professional body of coaches and was the first professional organization to measure competency and credential coaches. While other associations have developed credentialing systems for coaches and most coach training schools have a testing mechanism within their programs, the ICF's competencies and credentialing system remains the most internationally recognized. The competencies are available to readers in Appendix 1.

matter, communicate directly, and view the client as an equal partner and contributor throughout the coaching relationship. While many coaches may have some innate or natural talent in some areas, the ability to use all of the competencies easily and in a manner most suited to each individual client requires an initial investment of learning. The coach must undertake a course of development that allows him to find that initial connection of relationship with the client and to co-create a partnership with the client.

Getting Competence

> *"I know of no more encouraging fact than the unquestionable ability of man to elevate his life by conscious endeavor."*
>
> —HENRY DAVID THOREAU

Becoming a coach is a conscious endeavor that requires at least four investments by the potential coach:

- Attending a real and substantive coach training program over a period of time
- Engaging in a coaching relationship as a client
- Practicing the skills learned in the coach training program
- Understanding and accepting the underlying principles of the coaching relationship

Coach Training

There is no competence without training and learning from experienced coaches. It is absolutely necessary that the new coach find a training program that teaches coaching skills. The easiest way to find a good program is to enroll in an ICF-accredited coach training program or a program that holds the ICF-approved coach-specific training hours designation. These programs have been reviewed for both content and teaching quality. Such programs will require the new coach to leave behind old expertise and learn new skills. If a coach is not enrolled in or has not completed a high-quality coach training program, chances are she is not coaching, but is acting more in the role of a consultant or expert and is engaged in advising or counseling.

Being Coached

In order to understand both how to coach and the role of the client, the coach must be a client. Coaches committed to obtaining competence will invest in a coach of their own for a minimum of 6 to 12 months. This allows the new coach to experience how the coaching relationship unfolds from the client's perspective, to feel the power and challenge inherent in good coaching, and to learn coaching skills from an experienced and competent, if not masterful, coach. The concept and range of competency becomes much, much clearer to new coaches when they experience masterful coaching themselves.

The Necessity of Practice

Coaching competency cannot be learned simply by reading a book. Coaching is an interactive art based on the relationship of the coach and client. A coach who has completed a coach training program without significant time spent actually coaching will still be a beginner upon graduation. In order to know how to apply the skills learned in coaching programs, the new coach must obtain clients and practice the skills. Clients will receive value from the coaching even in these new stages of growth, and the coach will hone book learning into substantive and practical skills.

The Keys to Initial Competence

The coach's path to competence always requires some key shifts in attitudes and habits. The coach must move from expert to explorer, from leader to partner, from teacher to learner. That journey is easier and smoother when the language surrounding key shifts has been clarified by the coach. While each coach must find the language that will ring for them, the key shifts can be described as follows:

- *Being in full relationship simply because someone is your client*—Good coaches want to have a total picture of their clients: who they are, how they learn, how they work, what they want, what is their greatness, and what are their struggles. This curiosity arises out of a desire to use all that they learn as a coaching tool for their clients.

- *Believing completely in the client's capability to achieve*—The coach cannot trust the client if the coach does not believe in the client's innate ability to learn, grow, and achieve. If the coach has any doubts, the coach's hesitancy will become an unwanted party within the coaching space that will hinder the coach's ability to coach the client.

- *Treating the client as a powerful partner in the coaching process*—The coach considers the client an equal adventurer in the relationship. That means the coach must continue to seek and value the client's contribution.

- *Being an explorer, rather than a solver*—New coaches are often quick to offer solutions to problems or challenges. This strategy subtly, but effectively, negates the purpose of coaching. The client may get a quick answer, but rarely discovers a thinking process that will serve beyond coaching. Conversely, the coach who by nature is a master of curiosity and exploration allows the client to trust himself more fully as well and develop thinking and action structures that serve him long after the coaching relationship is over.

◆ *Being willing to accept that the client's truth is as or even more valid than the coach's truth, and then encouraging the client to choose—* Coaching is not a hierarchical relationship. If the coach regularly believes that she, as coach, has the solution or answer, then she is substituting her wisdom for the client's wisdom. In order to develop the client's abilities and strengths, the coach must honor the client's knowledge as equal to or greater than the coach's knowledge. The coach must also fully trust the client to choose what, in the moment, is right for the client.

Once these shifts become evident in the coach's relationship with the client, initial competence has been achieved. The coach is now prepared to get an ICF credential as a measure of competence. More important, the coach can now begin to grow that competence toward masterful coaching.

Growing Competence

> *"Improving competence involves continuing professional development. . . . That is really the crucial thing, not just passing an examination."*
>
> —Colette Bowe

The coach's growth toward mastery is evidence of continued commitment to competence. At the initial stages of competence, coaches are proud of new skill sets, using them well in service to clients, and are usually somewhat wrapped up in their own view of their coaching. This a natural place to be since the investment of time, money, energy, and emotion to get to initial competence is not small. In addition, most coaches have by this time gone through a risky career change from employee to self-employed or from a comfortable living to one that is less stable for the moment. In short, considerable changes have occurred. Therefore, a time for rest and celebration as well as recognition of the new skill set is appropriate and warranted.

That rest and celebration, however, is never long for the coach who is dedicated to continued improvement as a coach. These coaches truly recognize competence as change and advancement on a continuum of increasing capability. Thus, they undertake the three keys to moving toward mastery: supervision or mentoring, continued coaching education, and a broadening of coaching tools.

Supervision

Good coaches have their own coach for general aspects of life and business. Great coaches have a coach who coaches them on their coaching. Throughout their career, competent coaches should seek supervision from expert coaches. A coach seeking to grow competence should, on a regular basis, hire a master coach for supervision. It is imperative that the mentor coach hear actual coaching and comment on actual client sessions.[2]

Over the course of years, these mentors should come from different training backgrounds, use different coaching styles, and should have experience with different types of clients. In short, the competent coach seeks a broad variety of voices to observe coaching, give feedback, and suggest practices for growth. Supervision or

---

[2]Of course, the coach seeking supervision, in accordance with the ICF's code of ethics, must obtain a client's explicit permission to either tape a session for supervision or to have a mentor coach attend a session as an observer. If attending the session, the mentor coach should not interfere or comment in any way on the coaching during the session.

mentoring is perhaps the most assured way of growing competency toward mastery as well as maintaining the highest level of skill possible for clients.

Continued Coaching Education

No coach develops competency by relying solely on the foundational coach training received in the original coach training program. Mastery requires substantive graduate education in coaching and many hours of coaching clients. Significant workshops, conferences, and deep discussions with other coaches about the skill set underlying great coaching are the hallmark of the coach's yearly skill-building plan.

While continuing coaching education is required by the ICF to maintain a credential, the requirement should not be the driving force for the competent coach.[3] Instead, the competent coach seeks continuing education out of inherent curiosity that can only be satisfied by additional learning. Likewise, the coach affirmatively pursues continuing education to ensure that clients receive the best coaching she can provide. For competent coaches, the coaching classroom is a permanent part of their professional life.

Broadening Coaching Tools

The development of competence toward mastery also requires the coach to look outward beyond the coaching field. All truly masterful coaches have a broad knowledge base in many areas of self and workplace development. The purpose of this knowledge is not to make

---

[3]The ICF's requirement is a minimal 40 hours of continuing education over three years. In this author's opinion, that requirement is too low. Many professions have a base requirement of 20 to 30 hours of continuing education in any single year. This latter number is more in keeping with a significant growth of skill set rather than mere maintenance.

the coach an expert in a particular area, but to allow the coach to hear more deeply what is true for the client. Some areas of learning that can increase the ability of the coach to hear acutely, become more responsive to the client, and use coaching tools more effectively include: learning and processing styles, emotional intelligence, change cycles, leadership styles and behaviors, team building, language patterns (NLP courses, for example), and cultural differences.

Beyond such key areas of exploration, coaches growing from competence to mastery become keen observers of the outside world, particularly the world of language. Competent coaches work diligently to continually broaden their language bank and deepen their communication skills. They seek great language from the cultural world, from the world of politics, from their clients, and from those who inhabit their circle of family, friends, and professional colleagues. Books, movies, plays, the spoken word in all forms create additions to the coach's language bank. As language masters, they are then easily able "to choose the language in the moment that will have the most impact for the client."[4]

The competent coach moving toward mastery also becomes a zealous witness to coaching lessons found in surprising places. Books, movies, plays, television, interactions among friends—all become places of learning for the coach with lessons that can be used as coaching tools. Small lessons are noted; large lessons internalized. The analogies from life experiences and cultural gifts are filed for use in an appropriate moment. This sense of allowing the totality of experience to become the coach's learning playground is the default position of the masterful coach and the increasing habit of the competent coach moving toward mastery.

---

[4]This gift of access to language that has meaning for the client is described in ICF competency #6, Direct Communication, from which the quoted language is taken.

The importance of the continuum of competence, that cycle of growth that every competent coach must undertake, cannot be underestimated. Every measure of competence, whether imposed by the profession of coaching or by the agreement of client and coach, requires a continued forward momentum toward masterful coaching. Defining those measures is a task of critical importance to the coach, the client, the potential client, and the coaching profession as a whole.

Measures of Competence

> *"It is a fine thing to have ability, but the ability to discover ability in others is the true test."*
>
> —ELBERT HUBBARD

At some point, coaches who pursue mastery must submit to the measurement of their own competency. That measurement exists in two forms: the measure by the standards of the profession, and the measure of the personal barometer of skill that the coach develops and shares with his clients. The external and internal measures are not an either/or choice. The competent coach seeks and honors both.

External Measures of Competence

The profession of coaching, while relatively new, has quickly developed a significant series of methods for measuring competence. At the time of this writing, there were approximately 50 legitimate coach training programs within North America, and more worldwide. Most of these programs require some demonstration of actual coaching skill before bestowing the designation of graduate or a certificate of competency upon a student. At least two independent professional bodies, the International Coach Federation (ICF) and the International Association of Coaches (IAC), have developed credentialing systems requiring that the applicant pass a substantive skill exam to receive a credential. Those exams also require that the applicant's actual coaching be heard and judged by masterful, experienced coaches.

In addition, the profession has a body of educational institutions that give certifications as well. The competent coach will seek both external measures. Graduation from their coaching school of choice is evidence of successful completion of their foundational studies. Certification by an independent professional body gives the coach, as well as the public, a completely unbiased measure of skill that ensures both that the schools are training well and the student is learning well.

Internal Measures of Competence

The competent coach has a thirst to know that he is coaching well. In addition to the supervision mentioned previously, the competent coach engages in self-assessment and inquiry about the development of competence. This inquiry is not meant to be a fact-finding mission to identify faults, but a positive, qualitative measure of service to the client. The competent coach is also fearless about the measurement of her coaching, so much so that she invites the client to join in defining the measures of competency and the evaluation of whether the coach and the client together have achieved those measures. This type of conversation is one of the ultimate evidences of a deep and real partnership within the coaching relationship.

These internal measures of competency will vary in language from coach to coach since they are personally developed and adhered to. For competent coaches, the measures will, however, have common themes among them. Such measures will, for example, always emphasize the partnership between the coach and the client, they will always focus on the client's thinking and action structures, and they will require that the coach respect the contribution of the client to the coaching process.

Since the internal measures are personal to the coach and his style, there is no one format to follow. A sample format is discussed in the following. One of my favorite clients and I developed this set of measures by looking at the things the client principally enjoyed about the coaching relationship and what we together believed had produced some extraordinary results for the client. We used this list as a check to ensure that the coaching relationship still had a tone and tenor that served the client. In addition, if the coaching ever felt off-target we checked to see which of the measures was not being attended to. My client has since given me permission to publish the list here and elsewhere as an example of general measures of competency within the individual or group coaching relationship. Here are the measures:

- *Objective of high-performance coaching*—to assist clients to create new and more powerful thinking and doing spaces for themselves

- *Measures of coaching skills for co-creating powerful thinking spaces*:
  - The coach's invitation to exploration precedes and is significantly greater than the invitation to solution.
  - The coach is willing not to know where the coaching will go.
  - The coach and client create a light and safe atmosphere for exploration, experimentation, and challenge by both coach and client.
  - The coach and client create a space for contemplation and deeper thought.
  - The coach and client create a space for free sharing of each

other's instincts, feelings, and truths and feel privileged and gifted in that sharing.

❖ The coach and client become learners from each other and freely share that learning with each other.

❖ The coach and client connect past lessons to new learning and create continuity between the client's past, present, and future.

❖ The coach and client see the totality of the client, the client's growth in the coaching process and the client's growth in greatness, and continually relate that totality to creation of the client's future.

◆ *Measures of coaching skills for co-creating powerful doing spaces*:

❖ The coach and client create a space of focus and creativity that allows the client to identify, articulate, and be accountable for high-leverage actions.

❖ The coach and client create a space of informed risk-taking that allows the client to stretch the boundaries of what he has done before.

❖ The coach and client continuously hold and revisit goals so that the client's actions have direct impact toward specific goals.

❖ The coach assists the client to evaluate actions within a systems viewpoint, examining intended and potential unintended consequences.

❖ The coach assists the client to develop both situational and nonsituational decision-making criteria that will serve the client in determining what actions to take and when.

❖ The coach will assist the client in determining when action learning is called for.

❖ The coach will assist the client to create plans to achieve both immediate wins and long-term accomplishments that align with the client's desired external and internal results.

❖ The coach and client will assist each other in recognizing the time for change in goals, plans, or actions.

❖ The coach will assist the client in designing actions that leverage the client's strengths, way of being, and learning style.

❖ The coach and client will continually visit and integrate the learning gained from the client's actions and use it to design further action.[5]

As is evident, good internal measures are not conjured in a moment. Creating meaningful internal measures of competence requires the coach to undertake serious analysis of coaching performance. It also requires significant discussion with clients to ensure that the measures include the client's view as well as the coach's.

While external measures are important to the coach, internal measures of competence that are revisited and honed frequently become the heart of a coach's journey along the continuum of growth. Without this self-analysis and client feedback, the coach cannot be a significant contributor to discussions of competence either for himself or for colleagues. Lack of internal measures will severely limit or slow the coach's expansion of coaching skills, service to clients, and ultimately, the ability to help clients become great coaches for themselves.

Measures and the Profession

Besides being useful tools for the individual coach, internal and external measures are necessary to the profession as well. An industry that wishes to be recognized as a profession must be willing to define,

---

honor, and enforce standards of skill and ethics. It must also be able to clearly state the skill sets that make it different from other professions and define measures of those skill sets for its members that promote quality service to clients. A profession unwilling or unable to stand for a skill set that serves clients will fail to survive.

Individual coaches embrace the standards for the profession when they engage in external and internal measures of competence. Such engagement is critical to the public acceptance of and belief in the credibility of coaching and the recognition of a coaching profession. The continued honing of measures of competence increases the public's confidence in coaching as a contributive art and science yielding value to the consumers of the profession's services.

Thus, the continued growth and measurement of competency are critical to the profession's existence and expansion. Each individual coach shoulders a significant responsibility, either contributing by measuring competence or diluting public confidence by avoiding such measures. Legitimate coach training programs and the nonprofit associations that support the coaching profession must continue to push for acceptance and engagement in the measurement of coaching competence both to protect the public and ensure the public's ongoing use of coaching services. That commitment will become exponentially more powerful when combined with a commitment to ethical standards.

The Relationship between Ethics and Competence

"No amount of ability is of the slightest avail without honor."

—ANDREW CARNEGIE

Ethics and competence are symbiotic twins. True coaching competence cannot exist without the understanding and use of coaching

79

ethics. Coaching ethics cannot be palpably manifested without competence in coaching skills.

Competency, even at the basic level, requires an understanding of the limits of coaching. As suggested in other chapters of this book, there are issues, subjects, and areas that are beyond the bounds of coaching. These are sometimes referred to as the wrong container for coaching because they include conflicts of interest that may put the client's goals at risk. Also, there is conduct by coaches that may place the coach's interest above the client's. The use of technically good coaching skills in the wrong container or for the wrong reason is an unethical and incompetent practice by the coach. The competent and ethical coach remembers that he is first and foremost serving the client in a coaching relationship.

Conversely, there are ethical considerations that cannot clearly be emphasized if the coach does not competently use coaching skills. Recognizing a potential therapeutic issue requires a level of competence in coaching presence, active listening, and powerful questioning. Discussing a referral to another professional such as a lawyer, therapist, or consultant requires competence in trust and intimacy and direct communication. Helping a client determine what professional support outside of coaching might be best requires the skill of awareness. Thus, applying and holding ethical standards with clients in a way that serves the clients requires competence in technical coaching skills.

Therefore, any truly competent coach must fully understand the ethics of the profession and continue to develop competence to be able to completely apply and honor ethical standards. Ethics without competence and competence without ethics simply leave the coach open to either failure with the client, legal liability, or both. In a most basic sense, it leaves the coach unable to serve the public at the level clients deserve.

The Public and Competence

"I take all knowledge to be my province."

—Francis Bacon

The public has the right to knowledge about coaching and coaching competence. The profession and individual coaches within it have a duty and obligation to assist the public with means by which the public can determine competence with confidence during the purchasing of coaching services. No indicia of competence can guarantee that a coach will in fact be competent during the coaching relationship. There is, however, certain knowledge about coaching that the public can claim as its province with the assistance of the profession. For example, each individual coach can assist by frequently discussing measures of coaching competence. The purpose of these conversations is not to convince a potential client to hire you, but instead to educate potential clients about what competence should be in any coach they hire. In addition, coaches must be willing to be questioned about their own personal competence. This willingness to stand for the competence of the profession and your own personal competence will allow the public to make confident buying decisions.

To assist the public in hiring a good coach, many competent coaches have—and all competent coaches should have—a list of questions to share with anyone about competence. The questions that follow were developed with input from clients. While not a guarantee of certainty, they can assist anyone hiring a coach to determine whether the coach has a sound foundation and a commitment to ongoing development of competence. Critical questions for a consumer to ask include:

- Do you have a certification and/or credential? If yes, what organization awarded you the credential and what requirements or testing did you have to complete to receive the credential or certification?

- Did you attend a coach training program? Tell me about the content of the program. Is the program recognized by the national or international professional coaching association that is not related to the program?

- Define how you will work with me and what skill set you will be using.

- Define my role and work during the coaching process and your role and work during the coaching process.

- How do you explain or define your competence as a coach? What are the keys to that competence?

- What do you do to expand your skill set?

- Do you regularly get coached on your coaching or have supervision? What are the most important things you get out of that supervision?

- How do you set measures of success, and what is my role in helping set those measures?

- What is the last thing you did to measure your own competence as a coach?

- What is your greatest strength as a coach, and what coaching skill do you most need to improve?

Competent coaches will, in the majority, find these questions both exciting and challenging. They will not fear the questions, and will thoughtfully answer them. The comparison of answers from three or four different coaches will give the consumer knowledge to make a more informed choice based on the coach's current commitment to getting, maintaining, and measuring competence.

Conclusion

The hallmark of a great profession is the competence of its members. Coaches who are committed to being professionals demonstrate that commitment throughout their coaching careers. From their initial training to ongoing mentoring to being willing to be judged by their peers in a credentialing process, professional coaches use measures of competence to ensure that they are serving clients at the highest levels possible. That commitment combined with ethics, standards, and honor creates value for the public and for the community of coaches within the profession.

5

Developing and Maintaining Client Trust

Professional Focus, Clear Agreements, and Confidentiality

Dolly M. Garlo

Objective

The objective of this chapter is to identify the ethical and legal elements applicable to professional coaching that foster client trust. By developing and maintaining client trust, coaches can deliver excellent services and assist clients in producing extraordinary results in their lives and organizations.

Pre-Chapter Self-Assessment

1. Ethics and law both focus on doing the right thing, but ethical compliance requires self-enforcement, whereas legal compliance involves enforcement by others.

   a. True   b. False

2. Autonomy is an ethical principle that respects individual

choice; the principle of justice addresses consideration of community interests.

a. True   b. False

3. In law as applied to coaching contracts, *consideration* means the process of careful thought, deliberation, concern, and the exercise of high regard for others.

a. True   b. False

4. For a coaching-engagement agreement to be a valid contract, it must be put in writing.

a. True   b. False

5. Currently, worldwide, there are five professional coaching organizations with established codes of ethics and procedures to review claims of a coach's unethical conduct. All of these organizations are in the United States.

a. True   b. False

6. Coaching evolved primarily from the practice of psychology, and should be regulated similarly to the medical and health-care professions.

a. True   b. False

7. If a coach works with a minor as a client, the coach should get consent to do the work from an adult with legal authority and responsibility for that minor, and get agreement from both the adult and the minor about how the client's private communications will be handled.

a. True   b. False

8. A coach with a website and an electronic newsletter, who sells products through the Internet, does not need to worry

about privacy of consumer information unless also providing financial services.

a. True   b. False

9. Making an ethical pledge to clients to maintain the confidentiality of the information they provide to the coach will not prevent a coach from having to testify or provide coaching records in a lawsuit brought by a third party against that client.

a. True   b. False

10. The duty-of-care element in the law of negligence is grounded in the ethical principle of fidelity.

a. True   b. False

Introduction

Forming an effective coach–client relationship quickly, or ever, requires a foundation of trust. That principle is true in an individual, one-to-one coaching structure, and it is especially true in a group coaching context, in which the coach may work among a number of like-minded or similarly situated, but unrelated individuals, or with a particular related group in a workplace or organizational setting. Coaching is a professional-services business that focuses on *who* people are in the context of *what* they choose to do and *how* they choose to do it. A coach–client relationship characterized by closeness, empathy, understanding, and thoughtful and discerning compassion is crucial to the delivery of the professional service. This type of relationship enhances the ability of clients to learn, grow, make decisions, and take actions to develop, change, or create new experiences more effectively and expeditiously.

Development of trust is also significant for the coaching profession itself. The foundations of the profession include education and training, recognized levels of experience in identified competencies, certification of ability and experience by an independent professional body, membership and activity within professional coaching organizations, and an agreement to provide services in keeping with a code of conduct to which professionals in the field pledge their compliance. These attributes provide clients with an understanding of the purpose and practice of coaching, as well as a basis by which they can evaluate an individual coach's level of professionalism. Ultimately, this context supports the development and maintenance of client trust that is so crucial to the client's realization of beneficial results.

Choosing Professionalism as a Business Focus

Coaches assist clients to operate from authentic choice: to sort through existing challenges and opportunities, to expand upon the choices available to them, to prioritize among values to make the best choices, or to create new life or career designs based on those conscious choices. In addition, coaches might bring coaching concepts to individuals or groups in a workplace, or they may provide complimentary coaching in the community or to people who could not otherwise afford coaching services. Coaches likewise choose to provide coaching services in various forms: through their own businesses, either as a solo practitioner or as a member of a group of other coaches or professionals from other arenas; inside a large organization as employees or independent consultants; in an academic setting or through the provision of coach training to other coaches or members of the public. Recognizing the value of coaching, professional coaches also choose to be coached themselves.

One particularly important choice principled coaches make is to pursue their work ethically and with a commitment to continued professional growth. This choice sets them apart from others who are quick to adopt the business moniker *coach* without abiding by the hallmarks of professionalism designed to foster confidence in the profession as a distinct service. Those professional hallmarks include, at a minimum, the following practices:

- Making use of an established body of knowledge obtained by completing a minimum entry-level course of training from an educational body accredited to provide instruction that is commensurate with current standards in the field

- Committing to practice in accordance with a professional code of ethics, and agreeing to be held accountable for maintaining professional conduct

- Seeking individual professional credentialing from an objective body that can evaluate professional performance based upon demonstration of compliance with established standards

- Maintaining ongoing professional growth and development through continuing education

These activities foster client trust in the profession and in the individual coach. Tensions inherent in the business of delivering professional services can strain this trust. For example, when a client has achieved identified goals, or may be better served by another coach or type of professional service, a financial incentive remains for the coach to continue working with that client (continue doing business) rather than end the coaching relationship or make a referral (serve the client). In such cases, continuing to work with the client may not be directly harmful, but doing so may still not be in the client's best interest. The tension is between business (making money) and professionalism (satisfactorily serving the client and putting the client's interest first).

Other professional tensions might include how the coach addresses conflicts of interest or disagreement, protects the client's private information or identity, handles a client's proprietary information, gives or receives gifts or other compensation, makes third-party payment arrangements, or even whether or how the coach crosses the boundary from professional to personal relationship.

Professionalism answers to a higher standard—the coach's focus on the client's best interests. That focus maintains the integrity of the work as measured both by the client's trust in the individual coach and by the public's understanding of and trust in the coaching profession. A coach with a clear vision of coaching's professional foundation based on a high set of standards is fundamental. Such vision can prevent his practice from becoming a breeding ground for unethical behavior, which can both seriously erode a client's trust in the coach and cause the client to question the worth of coaching itself as a distinct professional service (Daigneault, 1996).

The Continuum between Ethical and Legal Professional Issues

In 1924, Lord John Fletcher Moulton, an eminent English judge, described *ethics* as the "domain of obedience to the unenforceable"— a continuum defined by a sense of duty and focus on the public good, which he noted involves "doing right where there is no one to make you do it but yourself" (Silber, 1995). Adhering to professional standards and a code of ethics that honors the client's needs and interests, and that focuses on potential concerns of the public served by the coach's work, may also ultimately prevent disputes and possible legal claims. Judge Moulton saw the law as mere obedience to the enforceable: Break the law, and you will be compelled by external forces to pay a price. Only after an agreement (such as work delivered within a defined set of standards) or other professional trust is broken is such external force required. The resort to such enforcement is unlikely if one operates from a higher professional sense of duty and a client-centered focus.

Stated another way, ethical behavior is a choice to conduct oneself in keeping with a set of core values, and the code of ethics of a profession is a form of self-governance defined by high standards based upon those values. "As the ethics of self-regulation [diminishes], . . . the law [rushes] in to fill the void" (Kidder, 1992, 2001).[1] The law rushes in to address concerns in the form of:

- *Private legal claims (civil litigation)*—Examples of private legal claims include contractual disputes or negligence actions based upon claims of failure to produce represented results.

- *Government oversight through industry regulation*—In many industries, regulation is addressed through business or professional licensing, a form of permission granted to the licensees to undertake a given practice. Such licensing exists to protect the financial or other welfare of the consuming public.

- *Criminal enforcement, if needed, to protect the welfare of the public*—Many criminal laws at both the national and state or provincial levels exist to protect consumers from theft and business fraud, and from major crimes and other inappropriate conduct such as abusive or exploitative practices.

Fortunately, the ultimate focus of coaching is on supporting the client's choice and best interests. In addition, early industry activities to define the coaching profession and its distinct pursuits included the development of a sound set of ethical principles to guide its undertaking.

---

[1]Based on a keynote speech delivered October 1, 1992, by Rushworth M. Kidder, founder and president of the Institute for Global Ethics, and former senior columnist for the *Christian Science Monitor* (content revised January 2001).

Maintaining Trust in the Client–Coach Relationship: Legal and Related Ethical Principles

As a relatively new profession, coaching has little written law governing or describing it—either legislatively developed, or as case law defined from courtroom resolution of disputes. The very nature of coaching and the role of the coach in assisting clients to take responsibility and create their own chosen results can prevent disputes and legal claims—so long as coaches exercise similar levels of responsibility for their work with clients, and do business in accordance with existing standards of ethical conduct in the coaching profession. Given these circumstances, however, much of what guides and governs legal issues in coaching must be derived from a study of how law has been applied to other professions, and from a determination of the ways in which coaching is similar to or different from those professions.

Coaching is unlike the legally regulated professions in law, engineering, and health-care and social-service-related fields, with their required high level of subject-matter expertise and greater potential for harm to the consuming public from substandard practices. Yet, coaching can derive considerable guidance from these professions.

Basic principles of contract law in business provide guidance for shaping coaching relationships and agreements. For example, the early developments of coaching as a distinct endeavor between clients and their business advisors or counselors underscored a desire, and even the need, to maintain privacy of communications. (See discussions about the historical development of the coaching profession in Chapter 1.) Concepts of negligence form the basis for legal evaluation of service delivery in various business activities and professional practices. In professions such as law, the medical and mental-health fields, financial services, engineering, and other similar undertakings, negligence is referred to as professional malpractice because the specialized nature of the subject matter requires an expert in the field to educate jury

94

members, as finders of fact in the trial context, so they may properly evaluate the relevant practice standards at issue in the dispute. By contrast, although coaching entails specific skills, approaches, and processes, the subject matter is more easily understood by people without specialized coaching education. Understanding something of both contract and negligence law and related legal concepts is beneficial for the professional coach.

Further, these legal principles rest firmly on ethical principles that already define the professional practice of coaching. See, for example, the International Coach Federation (ICF) code of ethics (http://www.coachfederation.org/eweb/). The former Professional & Personal Coaches Association (PPCA) was merged into the ICF (United States) in 1998 and contributed its established set of ethical principles for coaches. Thereafter, the ICF developed the coaching profession's first ethical conduct review process as a forum in which to address potential public concerns of unethical behavior by ICF coaches. A review of the other existing ethical codes for coaches may also be helpful. Each of the following professional coaching organizations has an established ethics code and conduct review process: the Association for Coaching (AC) (United Kingdom) (http://www .associationforcoaching.com/about/ethics.htm); the European Mentoring & Coaching Council (EMCC) (United Kingdom) (http://www .emccouncil.org/frames/aboutframe.htm; see "Downloads"); the International Association of Coaches (IAC) (United States) (http://www .certifiedcoach.org; see "IAC's Ethical Principles & Guidelines"); and the Worldwide Association of Business Coaches (WABC) (Canada) (http://www.wabccoaches.com/advantage/ethics.htm) (ICF, 2001; AC, 2004; EMCC, n.d.; IAC, 2003; WABC, 2003).

As previously mentioned, the important distinction here is on doing the right thing (ethics), versus merely avoiding the risk of incurring liability or defending against claims of liability (law). The resulting benefit for coaches who properly maintain compliance with established ethical standards is a *prevention* of legal liability. Basic ethical principles that underlie applicable legal doctrines include:

+ *Autonomy*—respect for individual choice
+ *Beneficence and nonmaleficence*—the duties, respectively, to do good and prevent harm
+ *Fidelity*—faithful adherence to truth and promises
+ *Justice*—a focus on community considerations

The very nature of coaching is grounded in the ethical principle of autonomy, since the relationship with a coach ultimately serves to respect and promote the client's unique choices. The coach's efforts are to exemplify beneficence and nonmaleficence in assisting the client to reach identified goals or outcomes. The coaching relationship embodies fidelity through the agreements the coach and client make about the delivery of services and the role the client plays in receiving and using those services. Finally, the coaching profession supports the concept of justice through the focus on individual and organizational growth and success, which ultimately benefits the communities with which clients and client companies interact.

Guidance from Contract Law

The legal concepts related to forming a *valid contract* are a good place to start discussing ethical and legal concepts related to coaching. That is because the first element of an enforceable contract is *real consent* by the people involved, such as an agreement for coaching services. Other elements include *competent parties*, also known as *legal capacity*; *valid consideration,* defined in the law as the exchange of something of value; a *lawful object or purpose;* and a *form* that is *recognized by law.* With these elements in place, the law will recognize an enforceable contract that allows the party who suffers from a broken agreement to receive some form of compensation.

Ethical principles are attached to each element of a valid contract:

- The contract itself recognizes the autonomy of people to choose what they value, with whom to work, and the manner in which to be in exchange with one another by making their agreement.

- The concept of fidelity is incorporated because contracts support adherence to promises made between the parties, through the required element of consideration and the enforceability of contract terms.

- The concepts of beneficence, nonmaleficence, and justice are integrated through the requirements
  - that there be real consent (a meeting of the minds, demonstrating that all parties mutually understand the subject matter about which they are agreeing, and that the agreement is not the result of fraud, deception, duress, undue influence, or coercion).
  - that the parties to a contract be people the law recognizes as legally capable of providing that consent (which excludes and thereby protects minors and persons disqualified by virtue of some legal disability).
  - that a contract take a particular form recognized by the community for enforceability (which may be implied in law by the circumstances).
  - that the subject matter of the contract is proper (that is, it does not address doing something fraudulent or unlawful, such as murder, prostitution, or gambling).

Clearer perspective on some of these legal elements of a contract and on real consent will further illustrate ethical principles.

Offer and Acceptance

Not every agreement between two or more parties is a contract. Typically, a situation in which one person agrees to do something as a favor for someone else (for example, an agreement to entertain at a party), or when the agreement is moral (such as an agreement to stop swearing) or social (such as an agreement to attend a church or community-service meeting) in nature, would not constitute a validly enforceable contract if that agreement was not kept.

Legally, a contract must start with a definite offer and acceptance of *that* offer. Responding to an offer with a change to or negotiation about what was offered is not acceptance, but such action may create a new offer, or counteroffer. For example, this situation often occurs in real-estate contracts when the buyer proposes different terms or a different purchase price, and the seller must agree to that counteroffer before the contract is considered binding. The buyer's response is not acceptance of what was offered, and the seller is still free to sell the property to someone else who accepts the original offer, unless the seller then accepts the buyer's counteroffer.

The offering party may also withdraw the offer before it is accepted, and a later acceptance does not create a contract because there was no longer a valid offer, even though the acceptance may then constitute a new offer. Although this differentiation may seem tedious, the distinctions are important and create the whole body of contract case-law interpretation, including whether an option to contract has been created, and other legal issues. Finally, the offer must be accepted by the person to whom the offer was made.

These contractual requirements of offer and acceptance illustrate the ethical principle of autonomy, emphasizing that people have the right to choose with whom they will work or do business, as well as the terms underlying that work. This underlying respect for choice also supports the notion that, for a lawful contract to exist, what is offered and what is accepted must match. Further negotiations may ensue until a clear offer is actually accepted, but until then, the parties are discussing possibilities and not contractual terms.

In a simple agreement to enter into a one-to-one coaching relationship, these distinctions may not be that important: the stakes consisting of a monthly retainer or hourly rate of payment are small, and the determination of whether the parties will work together in proper exchange (payment for services rendered) will be discovered quickly, thus limiting the potential harm from alleged breach of an agreement. The issues gain importance in protecting the various parties, however, when the relationships and agreements are more complicated, the related payment amounts are greater, or the terms and expected outcomes are more extensive, all of which might be applicable to a long-term, multiple-person, organizational coaching engagement.

Consideration

Offer and acceptance alone do not a contract make. There is a legal concept called *consideration* that transforms them into a contract. Legal consideration is not the process of careful thought, deliberation, concern, or high regard for others, as in the common English usage. In legal language, as detailed by the American Lawyer Media's *Law.com Dictionary* (2005), consideration is

> . . . a vital element in the law of contracts . . . a benefit which must be *bargained for* between the parties, and is the essential reason for a party entering into a contract. Consideration must be *of value* (at least to the parties), and is *exchanged for the performance or promise of performance by the other party* (such performance itself is consideration). [italics added.] In a contract, one consideration (thing given) is exchanged for another consideration. Not doing an act (forbearance) can be consideration, such as "I will pay you

$1,000 not to build a road next to my fence." . . . Contracts may become unenforceable or rescindable (undone by rescission) for "failure of consideration" when the intended consideration is found to be worth less than expected, is damaged or destroyed, or performance is not made properly (as when the mechanic does not make the car run properly).

Thus legal consideration is something of value bargained for and given up in exchange for a promise or another's performance. Consideration may come in the form of money, work, another promise, performance of an act, or abstention from doing something. Consideration may also be nominal, such as the contract term often included in a bill of sale or similar document that reads "for valuable consideration of $10 cash in hand received, the sufficiency of which is hereby acknowledged." As long as the consideration constitutes a bargained-for exchange agreed to by the parties, its value or fairness is not relevant to the valid existence of the contract. The combination of the offer, acceptance of that offer, and the existence of legal consideration creates a contract that is then supported by the ethical principle of *fidelity*, which requires that the parties adhere to the promises or agreements they have made.

Form of Contracts

Contracts are often written, although a contract may be unwritten or oral. Sometimes a written contract is required by law. An old English law enacted in 1677 known as the Statute of Frauds, which has been adopted throughout the United States and in many other jurisdictions, requires certain contracts, such as for the sale of land, leases with a term longer than one year, and similar important agreements, to be written and signed by all the parties to the contract. Contracts that violate the Statute of Frauds are not necessarily void, that is, they may be enforced, but rather they are voidable at the election of either party to the contract.

Whether or not a contract must be written, it is a good idea to reduce the essential terms of an agreement—parties, offer, acceptance, consideration, time for performance, form of payment, expected results or outcomes, responsibilities of the parties, and so on—to writing. Writing the terms of agreement honors the ethical principles of beneficence (doing good), and fidelity (keeping promises), and is an approach the community supports as reasonable (justice). Written contracts are also referred to as *express contracts*.

The existence of a contract may also be *implied*, another legal concept grounded in beneficence and justice that prevents the unjust enrichment of one party at the expense of another. For example, the existence of a coaching contract may be implied where there has been an oral agreement that consists of an offer for coaching services at a given price per month to be paid by the client, and the client has accepted that oral agreement by participating in the coaching sessions with that coach. If the client subsequently refuses to pay, the unwritten contract may be implied by the behavior of the parties. The contract is implied because the coach performed the services offered as consideration for the client's promise to pay, and the client accepted the offer by receiving the services. The ethical principles of beneficence and fidelity apply to protect a party who has benefited another with an understanding that the party providing the benefit would be paid. Justice (community interest) is served by uniform application of this concept. Difficulty may arise in determining and enforcing the terms of an oral contract—for instance, what was agreed upon regarding the length of the contract or the amount to be paid. Such vagueness leaves both parties with very little protection to support the application of the ethical principle of fidelity to their (alleged) relationship and agreements. So, while the legal concept of an implied contract may protect the parties' agreements so far as they can be determined from the circumstances, creating an express (written) contract serves both ethical and practical interests.

Legal Capacity and Real Consent

Real consent to a contract is mutuality of agreement—making a clear and definite offer, and having that offer affirmatively accepted with identified exchange of consideration for the agreement. But whether that consent is effective and the agreements are really mutual requires an evaluation of *who* the parties to the agreement are.

The parties to a contract must both possess *legal capacity* to enter into the agreement and create a clear meeting of the minds about the subject matter. That element addresses issues of potential misrepresentation, fraud, coercion, lack of representational authority (as when a person acts on behalf of a company or organization), or similar concerns that may call into question the binding validity of the contract. Legal capacity addresses issues of *competency* as well as *disability*, but in broader terms than we generally consider these topics.

Lack of competency may include impediments ranging from legal insanity, mental or physical incapacity, or intoxication, to marital disqualification and not having attained legal age. The capacity to contract is generally presumed unless one of these issues is called into question. These variables have different legal tests. For example, the classic legal test for insanity, which is declared only after psychiatric examination, is the determination that the person could not understand the nature and quality of his or her acts and did not know they were wrong, as first described in *Rex v. M'Naghten,* 8 Eng. Rep. 718, 722 (1843). Similarly, mental or physical disability may require a determination of whether the disability prevented a person from reading and understanding a will or a contract such that his or her execution of the document was invalid at the time it was done.

When any of the variables is called into question, a court may require official determination at a hearing that involves the person claimed to lack capacity, and this person must be represented by a lawyer. Capacity to provide real consent is typically determined by whether someone can understand the nature of the circumstances or decisions being made. Capacity may also be set by the law of a state or other jurisdiction, making it official that such capacity is lacking until, for example, a child reaches the age of majority in that jurisdiction. The age of majority or minority, also called *legal age*, is the age at which a person can enter into a contract or relationship, or take other legal actions. In the United States, this age is a variable generally determined by state law. While the age of majority allowing someone to vote is set at 18 by the Twenty-Sixth Amendment to the U.S. Constitution, different states may set the age of majority higher for some things (such as drinking alcohol or purchasing cigarettes) or lower for others (such as driving, getting married, or even consenting to sex).

Real consent involves making sure both parties, and particularly the party to be charged (the person who will pay for and receive a service or product), clearly understand what they have agreed to. In the coaching context, that may include what the professional coach will provide, under what parameters and timeframe, and with what expected results, and what the client will pay for and is expected to do. Coaches provide feedback, structure, process, alternative viewpoints, and sometimes suggestions, education, or advice. Clients, beyond simply keeping coaching appointments and having professionally determined services delivered to them, are expected to share, clarify, and revise their goals, choose a course of action, and then implement their plan to bring those goals to fruition. Coaching clients do not simply have professional services passively applied to them; they actively participate in making decisions, designing solutions, and, particularly, planning actions and implementing strategies to reach desired results. It is important that clients understand how all these things will come about, what part they play in determining their own course of action, and what the coach will or will not do.

In the realm of medicine and related health-care delivery, this concept of required understanding of the professional service to be received has been extended to create a duty of the physician to provide evidence that informed consent was obtained from the patient to be treated. For example, because of the complicated nature of the information one needs to understand to make medical decisions, getting a patient's simple consent, as in the form of a signature on a document, is not enough. The right to make one's own medical decisions or consent to treatment is legally protected by a requirement that the following elements of informed consent be addressed. The consent must be given by a competent adult (or must be exercised by an authorized agent who is a competent adult) based upon a physician's exercise of the duty to explain the recommended treatment, medication, or surgical procedure (including the expected results and side effects, risks, and potential risks, and those same expectations related to refraining from the treatment, as well as the reasonable alternatives), and then received before going ahead with the treatment.

The consent or agreement to receive other professional services that are more readily understandable does not bear the legal requirements of informed consent. Even so, to move forward with the services it may be advisable and good business practice to detail, in writing, the terms of the agreement between the parties (essentially a form of consent between them) to be sure it is clearly understood. That may include, for example, the length of service, the form in which the service will be delivered, expected results, payment amount and terms, confidentiality issues, how conflicts or disputes will be handled, and the manner in which the relationship will be terminated.

Additionally, coaches who work with children or adolescents will be affected by the need to contract for services with a competent adult who is authorized to consent to that work on behalf of those youths. As mentioned previously, for consent to be considered valid, legal capacity to contract involves one having reached a legally defined age for the activity at issue.

The concepts of legal capacity and real consent recognize the ethical principles of autonomy, beneficence, nonmaleficence, and justice. These legal concepts require that competent adults exercise their choice (autonomy) to obtain professional services, which encompasses the duties to do good and prevent harm (beneficence and nonmaleficence). These legal concepts also require that the rights of those who may not be fully capable of making a reasoned decision be protected from harm (again, beneficence). This application of ethical principles in the law supports the notion that a contract for professional services will not be considered valid unless a competent adult with proper authority engages such services on behalf of a minor or an individual who cannot fully understand the terms of the engagement or fulfill the terms fully (e.g., provide payment for the services). Legal capacity and real consent likewise support the notion of justice because the community benefits from the promotion and protection of fair dealings in business relationships between parties. All these ethical principles are also incorporated into the requirement that, for contractual consent to exist, there be a real understanding of the mutual agreements between the parties. Finally, legal capacity and real consent also provide the parties with the benefit of being able to legally challenge the contract or specific contractual terms that are not clearly set out and mutually understood, or to enforce those terms that are clearly stated and understood when a party fails to meet the agreed upon obligation. Adhering to these legal concepts supports the ethical notions of promoting good, preventing harm, encouraging adherence to promises made, and providing the smooth delivery of products and services valuable to the community.

Guidance from the Laws That Govern Privacy

Although for the coach to maintain the confidentiality of a client's information is considered ethical (the ethical standards of each coaching organization mentioned previously include a reference to maintaining the confidentiality of the coaching client's communications), no law mandates coach–client confidentiality, and little law legally protects confidential communications.

The right to privacy is an interesting legal development in U.S. law. The notion of right to privacy was first discussed by lawyers Samuel D. Warren and the future U.S. Supreme Court Justice Louis D. Brandeis in their article, "The Right to Privacy," published in the *Harvard Law Review* in December 1890 (Warren and Brandeis, 1890). Legal notions of privacy are related to the law that governs defamation, which provides legal protections against someone who makes false written (libelous) or spoken (slanderous) statements about another person that damage his or her reputation. Such actions clearly violate the ethical principles of beneficence and nonmaleficence.

Privacy law first expanded to encompass four general classes of civil claims for invasion of privacy, including:

- Appropriation of someone's name or likeness for one's own benefit.

- Intrusion into someone's solitude or seclusion, such as by invading one's home.

- Public disclosure of private facts; a claim for revealing particularly sensitive private information that would be highly objectionable even though it is true (such as income-tax data, sexual practices, personal correspondence, disputes with family or colleagues, health status) would not support a claim of defamation.

- False light in the public eye, which more closely resembles defamation. This is a statement that is harmful to one's reputation, even though the information may be generally true. In the privacy context, the harm is that the statement creates a false impression that is highly offensive to a reasonable person, which damages not just the person's reputation, but the expectation of being left alone.

In the United States, the developing law that governs privacy and confidentiality must be balanced by issues of constitutionally protected free speech, freedom from government intrusion on the rights of individual citizens, and due process, which encompass the ethical notions of autonomy, fidelity, and justice. *Due process* refers to a fundamental principle of fairness (addressing the ethical notions of fidelity and justice) that has been adopted by many countries. In the United States, the principle of due process applies to all civil and criminal legal matters, especially in court and similar legal proceedings that require clear notice be given about adverse claims and the accused person's substantive rights, and that require all legal procedures be followed for each individual to avoid prejudicial or unequal treatment. This concept is incorporated into the U.S. Constitution by virtue of the Fifth Amendment, which states, "No person shall . . . be deprived of life, liberty, or property, without due process of law" and is extended to all the individual states through the Fourteenth Amendment. (A complete version of the U.S. Constitution is available online at http://www.usconstitution.net.)

This body of law concerning privacy rights did not garner Constitutional protection until 1965, in a landmark U.S. Supreme Court case, *Griswold v. Connecticut*, 381 U.S. 479 (1965).[2] In that case,

---

[2]In *Griswold v. Connecticut*, 381 U.S. 479 (1965), the U.S. Supreme Court considered a Connecticut state law that made it a crime to provide information, instruction, and other medical advice to married couples concerning birth control. Under that law, Griswold, the executive director of the Planned Parenthood League of Connecticut, and her medical director had been convicted. On appeal, the Court

the Court concluded that while nowhere in the U.S. Constitution and Bill of Rights (Constitutional amendments) was privacy explicitly mentioned, when interpreted as a whole, along with particular provisions of the Bill of Rights, there must be a penumbral right to privacy that is Constitutionally protected. (*Penumbral* is a term previously used to describe the shadow cast during an eclipse between the part in full light and the part in full shadow. The term was incorporated into this case to refer to the existence of something whose boundaries are uncertain and inexact.) This case recognized the ethical principle of autonomy, acknowledging the rights of consenting adults to choose how to behave in the privacy of their own homes.

In 1973, however, the Constitutional right to privacy was tested in another landmark U.S. Supreme Court matter widely referred to as an abortion rights case: *Roe v. Wade*, 410 U.S. 113 (1973).[3] *Roe* was

---

was asked to consider whether the U.S. Constitution protected a right of marital privacy against state criminal penalties for contraceptive counseling. This was a landmark case because, upon inspection of the U.S. Constitution and Bill of Rights, no explicit right to privacy was found. The Court concluded that while the Constitution does not explicitly protect a general right to privacy, the various guarantees within the 1st, 3rd, 4th, and 9th amendments create a "penumbra," or zone, that establishes a right to privacy. The Court's decision recognized a new constitutional right protecting privacy in marital relations. Because the Connecticut law conflicted with the exercise of that right, the law was deemed null and void, and the criminal conviction was overturned.

[3]In Roe v. Wade, 410 U.S. 113 (1973), Roe, a Texas resident, sought to terminate her pregnancy by abortion, challenging a Texas law that prohibited abortions except to save the pregnant woman's life. Recognizing the case of *Griswold v. Connecticut,* the Court held that a woman's right to an abortion fell within the right to privacy, but the Court limited the exercise of the right to privacy in this context to the first trimester of pregnancy. The Court placed the first limitations on the Constitutional right to privacy by recognizing a different level of state interest for the second and third trimesters, to protect the competing rights of the potentially viable fetus. Subsequent cases have expanded these limitations, for example, to circumstances involving preventing suicide or disallowing refusal of a life-saving blood transfusion. In these cases, the claimed constitutionally protected religious freedom or privacy right is overturned considering the interests of third parties such as children (who may be losing a parent and therefore have a compelling interest in their staying alive) or the interest of the state which would be called upon to provide care for the children after the death of a parent from suicide or the refusal of treatment that otherwise might be considered a right of privacy or personal expression of religious freedom.

actually the first post-*Griswold* case to consider whether there are acceptable limits to the newly defined and interpreted Constitutional right to privacy. The Court concluded that limits do exist, and that the interests of other third parties must be balanced against an individual's right to privacy. This case incorporated the ethical concepts of nonmaleficence and justice, balancing them against the principle of autonomy. That is, one person's right to choose based upon his or her recognized right to privacy (in this case the mother's privacy right to decide what shall be done with her own body) may not outweigh the possible harm to the rights of another (the potentially viable developing fetus), which in turn represents the greater interests of the community that encompass all parties in interest.

Together, these two cases demonstrate the fluid (rather than clear-cut) nature of legally related ethical principles. Truly ethical dilemmas, choices made to address what ought to be done rather than what can be legally-compelled, similarly often do not have clear-cut answers, but must include consideration of competing interests and circumstances.

Laws in various arenas are beginning to extend privacy rights afforded to individuals' medical information (e.g., the Health Insurance Portability and Accountability Act, known as HIPAA, 2004).[4] These privacy rights are reaching into the realm of financial information (e.g., Gramm-Leach-Bliley Financial Modernization Act, 1999), particularly because of the expansion of electronic communication and storage of information.[5] In the United States, the

---

[4]In the United States, the Health Insurance Portability and Accountability Act of 1996 (HIPAA), which, among other things, intends to protect individuals with preexisting medical conditions or who might suffer discrimination in health coverage based on their health status, placed significant requirements on a variety of health-care providers and settings for protection of medical record information.
[5]The U.S. Gramm-Leach-Bliley Financial Modernization Act of 1999 serves to protect the privacy of consumer information held by financial institutions that are

Federal Trade Commission (FTC) and state agencies or federal and state Offices of Attorney General now focus on how businesses address consumer-privacy concerns and protect consumers' personal information through enforcement of legal prohibitions against unfair or deceptive trade practices. Consequently, many business websites post privacy policies that describe how consumers' personal information will be protected. Government legal actions have been brought against companies to enforce their promises in privacy statements related to the security of consumers' personal information, as well as for activities deemed unfair business practices.

Coaches who collect contact information from clients to send newsletters, workshop notices, or information about new products or services by email may also be subject to the FTC's privacy-related restrictions concerning spam (Federal Trade Commission, 2003).[6] (Spam is officially known as unauthorized commercial communication. For more information applicable to coaches, see http://www.coachfederation.org/eweb/docs/icf-ucc-spam-policy .pdf and http://www.ftc.gov/bcp/conline/pubs/alerts/whospamalrt .htm.) Those coaches who engage in e-commerce with online shopping

---

significantly engaged in financial activities. It requires the companies that offer financial products or services (like loans, financial or investment advice, tax preparation, debt collection, or insurance) to give consumers privacy notices that explain the institutions' information-sharing practices and give them the right to limit some—but not all—sharing of their information. While this law does not apply to information collected in business or commercial activities, other laws do apply to protect consumers, for example, those involved in online e-commerce transactions.

[6]The Controlling the Assault of Non-Solicited Pornography and Marketing Act of 2003, also known as the CAN-SPAM Act of 2003, was also enacted into U.S. law in January 2004, thus providing more specific guidance about spam, by requiring that *unsolicited commercial* e-mail messages be properly *labeled* and include *opt-out* instructions and the sender's physical address, and by prohibiting the use of deceptive subject lines and *false headers* in email messages. Similar legal prohibitions exist for commercial communications transmitted by fax. See http://www.spamlaws.com/ federal/can-spam.shtml for the full text of the law and additional information.

carts to sell products and collect electronic payments are well advised to address consumer protection laws and regulations. (See, for example, http://www.ftc.gov/privacy/privacyinitiatives/promises_educ.html.)

The ethical principles of nonmaleficence, fidelity, and justice apply to this area of a coach's business. The law incorporates consumer protection against harm from both certain privacy violations and harmful or deceptive business practices. In mandating that certain businesses provide privacy policies or follow certain guidelines for promotional communications, the law promotes faithful and consistent adherence to agreements by those businesses to further protect consumers, both benefiting consumers directly and promoting the public's perception of trustworthiness in the overall business community.

Claims of privacy violations are typically difficult and costly to pursue legally. It also is unlikely that privacy claims of a Constitutional nature or involving appropriation, intrusion, or false light would apply to the typical coaching relationship. A legal cause of action for public disclosure of private facts, however, is most closely related to the expectation of privacy that a coaching client may hold, particularly if the client expects the coach to keep the information obtained during coaching private. A betrayal of such a privacy expectation might include something as simple as revealing the client's identity to others in discussion or posting a client's name and comments as a testimonial in a marketing brochure or on a website without the client's, preferably written, permission. Such action might also serve as the basis for a negligence claim.

Such a client expectation of privacy may arise by virtue of a coaching agreement, contract, or engagement letter, or by the client's reference to currently published ethical principles of coaching, all of which address maintaining confidentiality of client information, as noted previously (ICF, 2001; AC, 2004; EMCC, n.d.; IAC, 2003; WABC, 2003). Violation of such an expectation may result in the filing of an ethical complaint with an applicable professional coaching organization.

Failure to properly observe other privacy and related consumer-protection laws may subject coaches to government-enforced legal actions, as well.

Guidance from the Law That Governs Confidentiality and Privilege

While *privacy* is considered a right to be free from unwarranted public dissemination of information, and even the right to be left alone to make one's own personal decisions (so long as these decisions do not infringe on the competing rights of someone else), *confidentiality* is a matter of entrusting another person with information intended to be held in confidence or kept secret. Confidentiality is born from a relationship between the party who reveals information and the party who receives it.

The law has long recognized the notion of confidentiality, particularly in relationships considered fiduciary in nature. The term *fiduciary* is derived from Roman law. In the context of a relationship between people, *fiduciary* means a person acting in the capacity similar to that of a trustee, wherein trust and confidence is involved, and scrupulous good faith and candor is required of the trustee toward the other person in the relationship. The term is often used to describe a person or institution that manages money or property for another, and that management gives rise to a requirement to maintain certain (often legally prescribed) standards of care, and to avoid imprudent behavior. (See *Black's Law Dictionary*, 1979, p. 563 and http://dictionary.law.com/default2.asp?selected=745&bold=||||.)

Examples of fiduciary relationships include doctor–patient, lawyer–client, principal–agent, trustee–beneficiary, parent–child, guardian–ward, and the like, in which the nature of the relationship creates a requirement to exercise the utmost degree of good faith (an ethical combination of beneficence and fidelity) by one party on behalf of the other. The legally recognized notion of confidential relations has been extended beyond those defined relationships to include relationships in which one person places confidence in another, providing the person confided in with a certain amount of influence that can be used at the expense of, or to obtain an advantage over, the confiding party.

Clients regularly reveal to their coach certain information that may not be appropriate to share with others, including business partners, employees, colleagues, or family members. This sharing is an important part of the coaching relationship that allows the coaching process to be effective, and it is an extension of confidence that puts the coach in a position of influence that could disadvantage the client if the coach misused or improperly revealed the information. Although maintaining confidentiality is not legally required, as discussed previously, good is done and potential harm to the client and her relationships is prevented through the mutual understanding and agreement that the client's confidences will be kept. Thus, confidentiality ultimately embodies the ethical concepts of beneficence, nonmaleficence, and fidelity within the coach–client relationship. The client experiences a professional relationship in which personal or professional information is discussed and kept private. The promise-keeping role of the coach is honored, and the ethical principle of justice is upheld, providing for public trust in the coaching profession overall.

In considering legal protection of confidential communications, however, it is important to differentiate between the concepts of *confidentiality* and *privilege*. The coach may ethically pledge to exercise confidentiality with client information, but still be compelled to reveal that information because the coach–client relationship is not legally privileged.

Legal privilege is governed by the law of evidence used in court proceedings; in the United States, legal privilege is governed by state law (Fed. Rules Evid. rule 501, 2004).[7] Typically, state law indicates that, unless otherwise provided, "no person has a privilege to refuse to be a witness; refuse to disclose any matter; refuse to produce any object or writing; or prevent another from being a witness or disclosing any matter or producing any object or writing" as evidence in court (TX Rules Evid., art. V, rule 501, 1998; FL Statute Title 7, ch. 90, § 90.501, 2004). States have recognized privileged relationships, including those of physician–patient, lawyer–client, husband–wife, psychotherapist–patient, clergy–penitent, sexual abuse counselor–victim, domestic violence advocate–victim, accountant–client, and others. It is important to note that, although some coaches may have backgrounds and even be separately licensed in these fields, the protection of privilege applies only to information collected from a client in pursuit of work in *that* field. Thus, despite one's background in another applicable field, if a professional is acting only in a coaching capacity, the privilege related to another professional field or license does not apply to protect the client's information.

This recognition of privileged relationships is for the protection of information provided by the patient, client, spouse, penitent, or victim, and is for his benefit, not that of the professional. Privilege provides that such individuals may refuse to disclose, and prevent any other person (e.g., the professional, staff, colleagues, or other consulting professionals brought into the matter by the professional on behalf of the client) from disclosing, confidential communications, including records that pertain to the purpose for which the professional relationship was established. The professional cannot claim privilege on

---

[7]See Federal Evidence Rule 501, available online at http://www.law.cornell.edu/rules/fre/rules.htm#Rule501, which states, in part, that "in civil actions and proceedings, with respect to an element of a claim or defense as to which State law supplies the rule of decision, the privilege of a witness, person, government, State, or political subdivision thereof shall be determined in accordance with State law."

her own behalf. For example, in a case brought by the client against the professional where privileged information is part of the client's case, the professional cannot refuse to provide information using the claim of privilege.

Even though nonprivileged coaching communications are kept confidential, they could be compelled into disclosure through a legal action brought by a client against a coach, or in action brought by a third party against the client. It is not unforeseen that a coaching client might become involved in some sort of legal matter (such as a business or even family law dispute) in which the relationship between the coach and client becomes known, and the confidential information or records the coach has gathered in the course of the coaching relationship are requested or compelled by subpoena. A subpoena refers to a court order to appear and testify, or, if it is a *subpoena duces tecum*, to appear and bring records. Failure to comply intentionally or without good cause is contempt of court, punishable at the discretion of the court by a monetary fine or even jail time.

Therefore, to honor the ethical pledge of confidentiality to a client, it is wise for the coach to consider just how much information and client communications to maintain in the form of paper or electronic (computer) records so that he can practically protect client confidentiality in the event revelation of that information is required. The coach may want to institute a business policy or practice about the types of information that will be collected, as well as how closed files will be maintained or destroyed (remembering that computer files may still be accessible after deletion). As unlikely a situation as it may seem, coaches can expect that they will be required to produce such records (including computer hard drives) in addition to their own testimony in a legal matter that involves their client.

Applicable legal standards state that generally a person may not testify to a matter in court unless evidence demonstrates that the witness has personal knowledge of the matter. See, for example, Federal Evidence Rule 602 at http://www.law.cornell.edu/rules/fre/rules .htm#Rule602 (Fed. Rules Evid., rule 602, 2004). Arguably, much of the information clients provide to coaches is not information about which the coaches have personal knowledge. Beyond information about which they have personal knowledge, testimony by coaches may be considered hearsay, and is therefore inadmissible. For example, see Texas Rules of Evidence 802 at http://www.courts.state .tx.us/publicinfo/TRE/tre-98.htm#RULE802 (TX Rules Evid., art. VIII, rule 802, 1998).

Hearsay is defined as "a statement, other than one made by the declarant while testifying at the trial or hearing, offered in evidence to prove the truth of the matter asserted." For example, see Texas Rules of Evidence, art. VIII, rule 801(d), 1998, available online at http:// www.courts.state.tx.us/publicinfo/TRE/tre-98.htm#RULE801. That is, if the coach repeats something that the client said, and that information is offered into evidence as proof of some matter asserted to support a legal claim, what the coach says is not a statement of the declarant (coach), but a statement of the client being re-asserted by the coach, and therefore is hearsay. It should be noted that there are a number of exceptions to the rule against hearsay as inadmissible evidence. Of particular importance is the exception that makes records or regularly conducted activity admissible as evidence, even though technically that information might be hearsay [TX Rules Evid., art. VIII, rule 803(6), 1998].[8] Therefore, the records made at or about the time of the

---

[8]See Texas Rules of Evidence 803(6) (available online at http://www.courts.state.tx .us/publicinfo/TRE/tre-98.htm#RULE803), which states that the following information is not excluded by the hearsay rule: "Records of Regularly Conducted Activity. A memorandum, report, record, or data compilation, in any form, of acts, events, conditions, opinions, or diagnoses, made at or near the time by, or from information transmitted by, a person with knowledge, if kept in the course of a

coaching work done with clients, and kept by the coach in the regular course of providing coaching services, qualify under this hearsay exception and may be admitted in a legal proceeding.

These legal applications, in furtherance of the ethical principle of justice, make it important for coaches, as part of their ethical pledge of confidentiality (beneficence and fidelity), to both understand and inform clients not only about how they protect the clients' information, but also about the limit to which that protection can be maintained. This is why the code of ethics of many professional coaching organizations includes an ethical standard for the coach such as, "I will respect the confidentiality of my client's information, except as otherwise authorized by my client, or as required by law." See also the International Association of Coaches (IAC) *Ethical Principles and Code of Ethics*, Section 4, "Privacy and Confidentiality" (http://www.certifiedcoach.org/about.html), which provides comprehensive treatment of these subjects, and states in the pertinent subsection, 4.04 Disclosures:

(a) *Unless prohibited by law*, coaches will only disclose confidential information if the client, or person legally authorized to consent on behalf of the client, has given express written consent. (b) Coaches may disclose confidential information without the consent of the client *only as mandated or permitted by law.* [italics added]

---

regularly conducted business activity, and if it was the regular practice of that business activity to make the memorandum, report, record, or data compilation, all as shown by the testimony of the custodian or other qualified witness, or by affidavit that complies with Rule 902(10), unless the source of information or the method or circumstances of preparation indicate lack of trustworthiness. "Business" as used in this paragraph includes any and every kind of regular organized activity whether conducted for profit or not."

Guidance from the Law of Negligence

An additional arena of law pertinent to ethical delivery of professional services is the civil tort law concept of *negligence*. A *tort* is a private or civil claim (as opposed to a crime or breach of contract) for which the law provides a remedy. *Negligence* has been defined as the omission of doing something a reasonable and prudent person, guided by the ordinary considerations that regulate human affairs, would do; or as doing something a reasonable and prudent person would have refrained from doing under the same or similar circumstances (see *Palsgraf v. Long Island Railroad Co.*, 248 N.Y. 339, 162 N.E. 99, 59 A.L.R. 1253, 1928). In professional malpractice, the reasonable person is replaced by the reasonable professional in the field, such as the reasonable doctor, engineer, or architect, because these professionals are expected to possess significantly higher levels of knowledge and expertise, which necessitates expert testimony to advise a jury on the standards of practice to substantiate a claim of negligence.

The legal elements of a negligence claim provide additional reasons for maintaining client trust. The law of negligence utilizes the reasonable person concept to establish a duty of care (beneficence) between individuals that fosters client trust in the relationship based upon work being done in accordance with established standards of practice. Those standards serve as a form of expectation or promise of quality exemplifying the ethical principle of fidelity, and become recognized by a professional community for the protection of affected clients (justice). Thus, these negligence law concepts mirror a profession's choice to develop a set of ethical principles to guide its members, like the codes of ethics in the coaching profession. In the law, a breach of the standards that causes harm allows the person harmed to legally seek compensation, which serves to support the promises or expectations the standards represent (further promoting fidelity). The legal structure likewise fosters justice by providing a basis on which the community can rely on the professional practice. With the coaching profession, the definitions of coaching and coaching professionalism set forth by professional organizations and training programs, along with their defined codes of ethics, must become that standard of practice that would be used in a negligence analysis, because negligence case law does not exist to define them. Those definitions and ethical codes, along with professional, ethical-conduct peer review, a form of professional self-governance, also provides the element of justice to a claim of breach of professional standards. If the coaching profession and its professionals continue to build on that foundation of ethical principles, there may never be a call to interpret the profession through the law of negligence.

Conclusion

Ethical principles are embodied in both standards of ethical conduct for coaching and the laws applicable to coaches. Fortunately, the nature of coaching, and the profession's early adoption and promotion of coaching competencies and ethical conduct standards will serve to minimize legal claims and litigation. Despite an absence of interpretive law that is directly applicable to coaching practices, legal concepts can provide important guidance. This legal guidance includes established requirements for valid and enforceable agreements, guidelines for protection of privacy, the ongoing interpretation of professional standards, and examples of fair procedures to follow when evaluating claims of alleged harm and potential ethical or legal violations. Because much of that legal guidance is grounded in basic ethical principles, coaches are wise to learn and understand the thoughtful and comprehensive codes of ethics that existing professional coaching organizations have established, and to consistently apply those codes in their professional relationships.

What lofty accomplishments, if coaching becomes the first

Case Study

You are a relatively new coach who, for the past year, has regularly taken free online courses that claim to address professional coaching skills and provide participant group discussions about how best to coach clients. You have completed college, having earned a degree in English with a minor in television and film. You were drawn to coaching because of your fascination with people and what makes them tick. You began actually coaching people in a one-to-one format about six months ago, and you started to charge money for your services last month. Other than service work as a restaurant host (you tallied the nightly dinner cash receipts and distributed the pool of tips to the other service staff), you have no other business background.

Questions

1. Where can you go to learn more about basic professional coaching competencies to make sure you meet or exceed clients' expectations?
2. What, if anything, will you be sure to include in your written coaching-engagement agreement or contract?
3. What are the hallmarks of professionalism, and how, specifically, will you demonstrate them in your work as a coach?
4. How does an understanding of the basic ethical principles of autonomy, beneficence, fidelity, and justice apply to a professional coaching practice? How does that benefit the profession of coaching?
5. How can you develop greater support for understanding and applying existing coaching codes of ethics in your client practices?
6. What, specifically, will you do to foster client trust in you as a professional coach?

profession in history to lack a body of case law developed from court decisions that resolved disputes about proper professional conduct or client agreements, and if the profession remains self-governed because it is built on an ethical, client-focused foundation. Attainment of such ideals must be fostered by development and maintenance of client trust in each individual coach and, consequently, in the coaching profession itself.

REFERENCES

American Lawyer Media (ALM). (1997). *Law.com dictionary*. Retrieved February 18, 2005, from http://www.alm.com/.

Association for Coaching (AC) (2004). *Code of ethics and good practice. United Kingdom*. Retrieved September 12, 2005, from http://www.associationforcoaching.com/about/ethics.htm.

Black, H.C. (Ed.). (1979). *Black's law dictionary* (5th ed.) (p. 563). Eagan, MN: West Publishing.

Controlling the Assault of Non-Solicited Pornography and Marketing Act of 2003 (CAN-SPAM Act) (2003/2004). S. 877 H.R. 2214. Retrieved September 12, 2005, from http://www.spamlaws.com/federal/can-spam.shtml.

Daigneault, M.G. (1996). *Ethics & professionalism: Why good people do bad things* [Electronic version]. Retrieved September 12, 2005, from Ethics Resource Center, http://www.ethics.org/resources/article_detail.cfm?ID=30.

European Mentoring & Coaching Council (EMCC) (n.d.). *European mentoring & coaching council ethical code. United Kingdom*. Retrieved September 12, 2005, from http://www.emccouncil.org/frames/aboutframe.htm.

Federal Rules of Evidence (1975). *Legal Information Institute (LII)*. P.L. 93–595, § 1, 88 Stat. 1933. art. V: Privileges, rule 501: General

Rule. Retrieved September 12, 2005, from http://www.law.cornell
.edu/rules/fre/rules.htm#Rule501.

———— (1975/1988). *Legal Information Institute (LII).* 1975, P.L. 93–595,
§ 1, 88 Stat. 1934; Mar. 2, 1987, eff. Oct. 1, 1987. Amended
Nov. 1, 1988. Art. VI: Witnesses, rule 602: Lack of Personal
Knowledge. Retrieved September 12, 2005, from http://www
.law.cornell.edu/rules/fre/rules.htm#Rule602.

Federal Trade Commission (2004). *Who's spamming who? Could it be
you?* Retrieved September 12, 2005, from http://www.ftc.gov/
bcp/conline/pubs/alerts/whospamalrt.htm.

———— (n.d.). *Privacy initiatives.* Retrieved September 12, 2005, from
http://www.ftc.gov/privacy/privacyinitiatives/promises_educ.html.

Florida Statutes (2004). The Florida Senate. Title VII, ch. 90, §
90.501. Retrieved September 12, 2005, from http://www.flsenate
.gov/statutes/index.cfm?App_mode=Display_Statute&URL=
Ch0090/titl0090.htm

Gramm-Leach-Bliley Financial Modernization Act (1999). 15 USC,
Subchapter I, Sec. 6801–6809. Retrieved September 12, 2005,
from http://www.ftc.gov/privacy/glbact/glbsub1.htm.

Health Insurance Portability and Accountability Act (HIPAA) of
1996 (2003). Public Law 104–191, 104th Congress, August, 1996
(last modified April 11, 2003). Retrieved September 12, 2005,
from http://hhs.gov/ocr/hipaa/.

International Association of Coaches (IAC) (2003). *Ethical principles and
code of ethics: Section 4, privacy and confidentiality.* Retrieved September
12, 2005, from http://www.certifiedcoach.org/ethics.html.

International Coach Federation (ICF) (2001). *International Coach Federation policy and procedure: Handling allegations of unsolicited commer-*

cial communications. Retrieved September 12, 2005, from http://www.coachfederation.org/eweb/docs/icf-ucc-spam-policy.pdf.

——— (2005). *ICF ethical guidelines. Part 3: The ICF standards of ethical conduct, confidentiality/privacy, no. 22*. Retrieved September 12, 2005, from http://www.coachfederation.org/eweb/Dynamic Page.aspx?Site=ICF&WebKey=3087def4-f88f-4426-9cc6-ca692c 4a900c.

Kidder, R.M. (2001). There's only ethics . . . *Institute of Global Ethics*. Retrieved February 18, 2005, from http://www.globalethics.org/corp/keynotes.html.

Silber, J. (1995). Obedience to the unenforceable. *The New Criterion 13*(10). Retrieved February 18, 2005, from *Roe v. Wade*, 410 U.S. 113 (1973)" http://www.newcriterion.com/archive/13/jun95/silber.htm.

Texas Rules of Evidence (1998). Art. V: Privileges, rule 501: Privileges recognized only as provided. Retrieved September 12, 2005, from http://www.courts.state.tx.us/publicinfo/TRE/tre-98.htm#RULE501.

——— Art. VIII: Hearsay, rule 801: Definitions, (d), Hearsay. Retrieved September 12, 2005, from http://www.courts.state.tx.us/publicinfo/TRE/tre-98.htm#RULE801.

——— Art. VIII: Hearsay, rule 802: Hearsay rule. Retrieved September 12, 2005, from http://www.courts.state.tx.us/publicinfo/TRE/tre-98.htm#RULE802.

——— Art. VIII: Hearsay, rule 803: Hearsay exceptions, availability of declarant immaterial, (6) records of regularly conducted activity. Retrieved September 12, 2005, from http://www.courts.state.tx.us/publicinfo/TRE/tre-98.htm#RULE803.

Warren, S.D., & Brandeis, L.D. (1890). The right to privacy. *Harvard Law Review 4*(5), 193–220. Retrieved September 12, 2005, from

http://www.lawrence.edu/fast/boardmaw/Privacy_brand_warr2
.html.

Worldwide Association of Business Coaches (WABC) (2003). *Worldwide Association of Business Coaches code of business coaching ethics and
integrity*. Sidney, BC, Canada. Retrieved September 12, 2005,
from http://www.wabccoaches.com/advantage/ethics.htm.

6

Multiple-Role Relationships in Coaching

Ofer Zur and Sharon K. Anderson

Objective

As an emerging profession, coaching is facing the challenge of identi-fying, articulating, and guiding its practitioners in how to deal with wide-ranging areas of ethical issues, including dual relationships. This chapter defines multiple-role relationships, describes the different types of dual relationships that might take place between a coach and a client, provides examples, and discusses three professional coaching association ethics codes as they relate to multiple-role relationships. Additionally, this chapter provides guidelines for establishing and maintaining ethical coaching in multiple-role relationships.

Pre-Chapter Self-Assessment Test

1. Multiple-role relationships with a client in a coaching context means the coach has more than just a professional relationship with the client.

    a. True   b. False

2. If a coach tries hard enough, she can and should avoid all multiple-role relationships with current clients.

    a. True   b. False

3. Multiple-role relationships, even if they create a conflict of interest, are ethical for the coach to enter into as long as both parties understand the conflict of interest.

    a. True   b. False

4. A dual role is exploitive in nature when the coach seeks to benefit himself.

    a. True   b. False

5. Multiple-role relationships in coaching are normal and helpful because in life we have many roles with people who are potential clients.

    a. True   b. False

6. Multiple-role relationships with coaching clients are different from multiple-role relationships with therapy clients.

    a. True   b. False

7. A sexual relationship with a coaching client might be considered ethically awkward but not unethical.

    a. True   b. False

Defining Multiple–Role Relationships

In life, we all hold various roles—spouse, parent, adult, child, employee, employer, and so on. In coaching, the coach sometimes holds more than just the coaching role with the client. When this happens, the coach is in a dual or multiple-role relationship with the client. Examples of multiple-role relationships are when a coach's client is also the coach's student, friend, employee, fellow church or congregational member, gym mate, family member, employer, business associate, teammate in a local recreational league, co-business investor, or fellow member in the local Chamber of Commerce or Rotary Club. Multiple-role relationships can also include situations in which different clients of the same coach are friends, colleagues, business associates, or business competitors. Additionally, dual relationships occur when a coach shops at the shoe or grocery store that her client owns, when a coach is on a committee or board with a client, or when their children attend the same school or play on the same little league team.

Multiple-role relationships can be *concurrent* or *sequential* (Kitchener, 2000; Lazarus & Zur, 2002; Pope & Vasquez, 1998). When coaches are involved in a business relationship, friendship, or any other multiple-role relationship with their clients as the coaching is taking place, these relationships constitute concurrent dual relationships. When coaches and clients first end the coaching relationship and then start a new business venture, social engagement, friendship, or any other relationship, these relationships constitute sequential dual relationships. Nonsexual, nonexploitative dual relationships between a coach and a client in and of themselves are not unethical. An exploitative relationship creates a relationship where the coach takes advantage of the client or selfishly uses the relationship for the coach's own end. In fact, there are no ethical injunctions against sexual or nonsexual sequential dual relationships with former clients as long as those relationships are nonexploitative. However, sexual dual relationships with current clients are ill advised and always unethical.

Multiple-Role Relationships in Coaching

Although much has been written about and debated in the psychotherapeutic literature about dual relationships, very little has been explored about multiple-role relationships in the coaching profession (Kitchener, 2000; Lazarus, 1994; O'Laughlin, 2001; Pope & Vasquez, 1998; Sonne, 1994). In the psychotherapy literature, psychotherapists seem to be varied in their attitude toward dual relationships. On one side of the debate are those who view almost all dual relationships as problematic and even harmful, and they therefore advocate adhering to rigid and rather inflexible boundaries (Koocher & Keith-Spiegel, 1998; Pope & Vasquez, 1998; Simon, 1991). This perspective possibly stems from psychoanalytic tradition, the desire to protect patients from predatory therapists, and encouragement from within the profession to consider risk-management practices. On the other side of the debate are those who acknowledge that dual relationships are basically normal and natural to the human condition, that such relationships are unavoidable in many settings, such as rural or business communities, and who view dual relationships as potentially helpful when they are implemented appropriately (Lazarus & Zur, 2002; Zur, 2000). Within the psychotherapeutic community, there seems to be a clear shift toward the latter view of dual relationships. In response to a growing awareness that many multiple-role relationships are indeed helpful and often unavoidable in small or rural communities and small organizations, the American Psychological Association recently clarified via its 2002 *Ethical Principals of Psychologists and Code of Conduct* that "Multiple relationships that would not reasonably be expected to cause impairment or risk exploitation or harm are not unethical" (2002, p. 6).

Overall, the nature of dual or multiple-role relationships in the context of coaching is very different from dual or multiple-role relationships in psychotherapy. These differences are the heart of what separates coaching from psychotherapy. The focus of coaching is on health, wellness, future, and growth rather than on pathology, brokenness, and the past. Clients who seek coaching generally tend to be more functional and significantly less pathological or mentally ill than psychotherapy patients (Williams & Davis, 2002). The coach–client relationship is a co-creative, equal relationship. The fact that coaching is geared to the functional population probably also means that the power differential between coaches and clients is less than in psychotherapy, or does not exist at all, and therefore the chance of coaches exploiting clients is significantly lower.

Dual and Multiple-Role Relationships in Coaching

In many settings, multiple-role relationships are viewed as the norm. Groups of like-minded people, or folks with similar lifestyles, come together in rural communities, churches, and small-business communities; and urban locals come together for a sense of community. Mutual reliance, interdependence, employment of those familiar with duality—all these characteristics are often what help such communities function, survive, and thrive. Regardless of the settings, many clients probably choose their coaches only after they get to know, appreciate, and respect those persons in their churches, clubhouses, boardrooms, or business clubs.

The scope of dual relationships in coaching is as wide as the coaching profession itself. Dual relationships can occur in personal coaching to business coaching, leadership coaching, and even in some specialties such as relationship coaching or parenting coaching. Because of these various relationships, coaches may find themselves actually expected to socialize, play golf, and relate with clients outside of the coaching sessions. Such interaction is even expected in corporate or executive coaching because much of the coaches' role is to attend corporate functions and meetings, as well. Dual relationships are more likely to be accepted in coaching, which generally serves the more functional and emotionally healthy population than psychotherapy. But one should still be cautious and clear that the relationship with clients outside of the coaching relationship is not disruptive, harmful, or misinterpreted.

Following are some examples of dual relationships in coaching:

- Business clubs, such as Rotary or Chamber of Commerce, are designed to introduce the membership to local resources and fellow businesspeople, including accountants, attorneys, marketers, or coaches. Dual relationships are frequent in such organizations because members often also consult, co-invest, and are involved in a variety of ways in each other's businesses.

- Coaches who work with athletes often share a passion with those athletes for the same sports. Sharing that passion often translates to sharing the tennis or basketball court, gym, or pool.

- Clients look for personal or business coaches in the same way they search for a marketing consultant, accountant, or attorney. Therefore, sophisticated clients are less likely to pick their coaches from TV or Web ads than from a proven referral by a trusted friend or respected business associate. Dual relationships also occur when friends, colleagues, or business associates share a coach.

- When a personal coach has helped a client develop a new business, the relationship shifts from a personal coach position to that of an organizational coach, in which the coach works with the entire organization or becomes a consultant or shareholder. This evolution constitutes a sequential dual relationship.

♦ Ethnic minority, gay, lesbian, or disabled clients are often inclined to choose a coach, especially a successful one, who shares their culture, sexual orientation, or disability because they trust the coach, whom they often know from the community.

Dual Relationships as the Norm in Business

Coaches often work with businesspeople, who are generally accustomed to dual relationships. Dual relationships are the norm in business in the United States and the world in general because people in business often are part of a family business in which blood and money are intermixed and duality is the rule. The Family Enterprise Center (FEC) reports that family-owned businesses comprise more that 80 percent of all business enterprises in North America, 60 percent of the total U.S. employment, 78 percent of all new jobs, and 65 percent of all wages paid (2004).

The Ethics of Dual Relationships in Coaching

Generally, all codes of ethics of major coaching organizations, such as those of the International Association of Coaches (IAC, 2005) and the International Coach Federation (ICF, 2005), have sections emphasizing the importance of respect for clients' dignity, autonomy, and privacy. Although the terms *dual relationships* or *multiple relationships* are not mentioned in any of the codes, conflict of interest, unfair discrimination, exploitation, misuse of power, and influence are addressed. Following is a review of the stance of the major organizations' codes of ethics on nonsexual dual relationships, sexual dual relationships, and bartering.

Conflict of Interest

Concerns with conflict of interest seem to be the focus of all major coaching organizations. The IAC's "Ethical Principles and Code of Ethics" includes a section on conflicts of interest, which includes the following:

(a) Whenever feasible, a coach refrains from taking on professional obligations when preexisting relationships would create a risk of conflict of interest.

(b) If a coach finds that, due to unforeseen factors, a potential conflict of interest relationship has arisen, the coach attempts to resolve it with due regard for the best interests of the affected person and compliance with the Ethics Code.[1]

The ICF code of ethics includes a similar section on conflicts of interest, which states the following:

25. I will seek to avoid conflicts between my interests and the interests of my clients.

26. Whenever any actual conflict of interest or the potential for a conflict of interest arises, I will openly disclose it and fully discuss with my client how to deal with it in whatever way best serves my client.

27. I will disclose to my client all anticipated compensation from third parties that I may receive for referrals or advice concerning that client.[2]

---

[1]International Association of Coaches (IAC) (2005). Conflict of interest. *Ethical principles and code of ethics*.
[2]*Ibid*

Sexual Dual Relationships

All coaching codes of ethics (e.g., the IAC's 2005 "Ethical Principles and Code of Ethics," and the 2005 "ICF Code of Ethics") are unified in that sexual relationships with current clients are always unethical. IAC code simply states in section 3.04 that "Coaches agree not to be sexually involved with current clients."[3] ICF Principle #11 states "I will not become sexually involved with my clients." Additionally, IAC section 1.16, paragraph (b), states that

> Coaches do not engage in sexual relationships with personnel over whom the coach has evaluative or direct authority, because such relationships may be viewed as exploitative.[4]

Bartering

In regard to bartering, IAC code section 1.15 and ICF standard #28 states that

> A coach may participate in bartering only if the relationship is not exploitative. Coaches are free to negotiate accepting goods, services, or other nonmonetary remuneration in return for coaching services, within the legal and income tax limitations of the country of practice.[5]

Conclusion

Nonsexual dual relationships in coaching do not necessarily lead to exploitation, nor are they automatically unethical or illegal. In fact, in some contexts (for example, in rural areas or small social/ethnic/

---

[3]Ibid., section 304.
[4]Ibid., section 1.16, paragraph (b).
[5]Ibid., section 1.15.

business communities), dual or multiple-role relationships for coaches are unavoidable. Almost all professional mental-health ethical guidelines recognize this duality and therefore do not mandate a blanket avoidance of dual relationships. However, all guidelines do prohibit sexual dual relationships, exploitation, and harm of clients. In addition, the ICF code of ethics addresses conflict of interest and states that "Whenever any actual conflict of interest or the potential for a conflict of interest arises, I will openly disclose it and fully discuss with my client how to deal with it in whatever way best serves my client." Therefore, we encourage coaches to be sensitive to and aware of situations that might lead to an exploitative relationship. Some client factors may deter a coach's decision to enter into another relationship with that client, while other factors might suggest that a relationship in addition to the professional relationship is reasonable and even beneficial to the client. Some of these factors include the client's culture, age, social position and community life, maturity, life experience, vulnerability to the coach's influence (e.g., the client is not able or willing to debate and challenge the coach), and the client's degree of comfort with dual-role complexities.

If you see that a nonsexual, dual-role relationship is likely to occur, and you have considered the factors mentioned previously, your next step is to think through the following series of questions. Before we share those questions, we would encourage you to consult with another coach (more specifically, a senior coach), or possibly an attorney. The consult can help illuminate any blind spots that you may have or any considerations you may not have thought about. During the consultation, you might discuss the following questions:

- What impact will entering this dual-role relationship have on the welfare of my client? Will it benefit the client?

- Are there any potential or actual conflicts of interest in entering this dual-role relationship?

- Will, or how might, my coaching effectiveness be enhanced or compromised by entering this dual-role relationship? Along this same line, will or could my professional judgment be improved or impaired if I enter this other relationship?

- What is the likelihood for harm or exploitation of my client if we enter this other relationship while still engaged in the coaching relationship?

As previously mentioned, a dual-role relationship can be sequential, too (you have officially ended your coaching relationship and now, for example, there is an opportunity to engage in a business relationship or social relationship with your former client). You may wish to think through the questions previously identified in case this person wishes to resume coaching work with you in the future. Again, we encourage you to consult with a senior coach, someone who has likely dealt with similar issues before, and who can help you think through any possible conflicts. For certain, whether this is a possible concurrent or sequential dual relationship, you and your client need to talk about the complexities, richness, potential benefits, and drawbacks that may arise from such a relationship.

Case Study

Jim Adams is a coach who lives and works in a midwestern town with a population of approximately 100,000. He is approached by a neighbor with whom he has been very friendly for about 20 years. The neighbor indicates that he and his family members are all going through a number of changes in their lives. The neighbor states that he trusts Jim and wants to hire him as a coach to assist with some personal issues and finding a new

(Continued)

job. The neighbor also states that one of his daughters seems unable to decide what to do with her life upon graduation from college. He requests that Jim also coach the daughter for which the neighbor will pay.

Questions

1. Should Jim take on the coaching of a friend and neighbor?
2. If Jim decides to coach his neighbor, can he also coach the neighbor's daughter?
3. Are there any safeguards that Jim should set up if he should take the daughter on as a client?
4. What should Jim do if his neighbor wants to know information about his daughter's coaching session?
5. Should Jim accept payment from the father or encourage the daughter to pay for her own services? Why?

REFERENCES

American Psychological Association (APA) (2002). Ethical principles of psychologists and code of conduct. *American Psychologist 57*, 1060–1073.

Family Enterprise Center (2004). Statistics presented in introductory information on website. Retrieved September 12, 2005, from http://64.226.232.47/fec/.

International Association of Coaches (IAC) (2005). *Ethical principles and code of ethics.* Retrieved September 12, 2005, from http://www.certifiedcoach.org/ethics.html.

International Coach Federation (ICF) (2005). *The International Coach Federation code of ethics.* Retrieved September 12, 2005, from http://www.coachfederation.org/eweb/.

Kitchener, K.S. (2000). *Foundations of ethical practice, research, and teaching in psychology.* Mahwah, NJ: Lawrence Erlbaum.

Koocher, G.P., & Keith-Spiegel, P. (1998). *Ethics in psychology: Professional standards and cases.* New York: Oxford University Press.

Lazarus, A.A. (1994). How certain boundaries and ethics diminish therapeutic effectiveness. *Ethics & Behavior 4*(3), 255–261.

Lazarus, A.A., & Zur, O. (2002). *Dual relationships and psychotherapy.* New York: Springer.

O'Laughlin, M.J. (2001). Dr. Strangelove: Therapist-client dual relationship bans and freedom of association, or how I learned to stop worrying and love my clients. *University of Missouri at Kansas City Law Review 69*, 697–731.

Pope, K.S., & Vasquez, M.J.T. (1998). *Ethics in psychotherapy and counseling: A practical guide.* San Francisco: Jossey Bass.

Simon, R.I. (1991). Psychological injury caused by boundary violation precursors to therapist-patient sex. *Psychiatric Annals 21,* 614–619.

Sonne, J.L. (1994). Multiple relationships: Does the new ethics code answer the right questions? *Professional Psychology: Research and Practice, 25,* 336–343.

Williams, P., & Davis, D.C. (2002). *Therapist as life coach: Transforming your practice.* New York: Norton.

Zur, O. (2000). In celebration of dual relationships: How prohibition of non-sexual dual relationships increases the chance of exploitation and harm. *Independent Practitioner 20*(3), 97–100.

7

Ethical Use of Assessments in Coaching

Debra Robinson

Objectives

This chapter explores the issues associated with using assessments in coaching. There are many assessment tools on the market today; therefore, the savvy coach needs to be aware of the range of tools available, and to know when and how to use them appropriately.

A variety of ethical issues revolves around the use of assessments. Consequently, one must have training and corresponding credentials to purchase and use many high-quality assessment tools. Becoming qualified to use an assessment tool often requires successful completion of a certification program or even more extensive education and training. Continued learning and practice are necessary to become an expert with any assessment tool.

Pre-Chapter Self-Assessment Test

1. Every coaching engagement should include an assessment tool.

   a. True   b. False

2. All coaches are equally qualified to conduct assessments.

   a. True   b. False

3. Most leadership-development programs incorporate assessment tools.

   a. True   b. False

4. One should consider test reliability and validity when using an assessment tool.

   a. True   b. False

5. Emotional-intelligence factors separate exceptional leaders from average performers.

   a. True   b. False

6. If you are going to use an assessment tool, reading the test manual is a good idea.

   a. True   b. False

7. Successful completion of an assessment-tool certification course is required to purchase and use many assessment tools.

   a. True   b. False

8. Participation in an assessment-tool certification course is all a coach needs to be an expert with the tool.

   a. True   b. False

9. The feedback process is critical to effectively use assessment tools.

   a. True   b. False

10. Clients may bring assessment results to their coach that they received in other settings.

    a. True   b. False

Introduction

When we hear the word *assessment*, we generally think of a standardized tool. Many standardized assessment tools are used today because assessments can provide valuable information in coaching relationships. However, coaches need to know what information they are seeking, and why they are using a particular tool.

For example, assessments can help elicit client information quickly, and even serve as a conversation starter in a coaching session. Many leadership-development programs use assessments as a foundation for executive-development planning and coaching. An assessment tool or process may even be the trigger to get someone into coaching. For example, a person seeking career coaching is likely to request some type of assessment. Most clients have used an assessment tool somewhere before being coached, and so they are likely to have feelings about assessment tools and the process. By reviewing some general assessment practices used in coaching relationships, you can better understand how to most effectively use other standardized assessment tools in coaching.

Coaches regularly engage in assessment processes. Many coaches use some type of *intake assessment* with new clients. This assessment may be a data form that seeks clients' background information, their previous coaching relationships, and their needs and expectations for coaching. This process lets clients immediately provide some personal background information and requires them to think about their goals for the coaching relationship. Some coaches use *process assessments* after sessions or at regular intervals to examine what is and is not working in the coaching relationship. This process allows for adjustments and can help keep clients fully engaged in the coaching relationship. Some coaches do an assessment when they complete a coaching engagement. This assessment provides reflection for the client, feedback for the coach, and helps to symbolize the end of the coach–client relationship.

As you consider the information you seek from your clients through the intake, process, and closure assessments, ethical guidelines come into play. This chapter explores types of assessments and the issues that contribute to ethical assessment practices.

Levels of Assessments and Ethical Practices

We can consider assessments at three different levels: organizational, group, and individual (APA, 2004). Let us look at these levels and the relevant ethical issues in more detail.

Organizational Assessments

Organizational-level assessments may focus on the business climate, culture, attitudes, and values; workforce issues; and employee satisfaction and needs. These assessments might be used for planning strategically, determining benchmark strengths and desired leadership competencies, gauging employee success with quality initiatives, and forecasting future employment needs. Or some community groups and churches, for example, might use organizational-level assessments to determine member satisfaction and needs.

Whatever the level of assessment, as a coach you must remember some key ethical practices:

- Focus on questions that are relevant to the issues and goals of coaching

- Determine in advance how you will use the assessment information, and with whom you will share it. Organizational-development interventions, for instance, often include sharing all responses without attribution to a particular person.

Most coaches do not direct assessment projects at the organizational level; organizational consultants usually do this work. Coaches, however, are likely to have individual clients whose company is undergoing organizational assessments. These individuals may seek coaching because of personal issues or group-interaction issues that surfaced during an organizational assessment. Coaches can then help these clients explore their concerns and the underlying processes to gain a higher level of understanding of themselves, their work unit, and the broader organization.

Group Assessments

Group-level assessments generally focus on team development and work-group issues. You might use individual assessments and incorporate group exercises to help team members appreciate styles and competencies other than their own. A common focus of group-level assessments is on enhancing communication and working through conflict issues. Deeprose (1995) uses a team-coach model to promote management skill development in team leaders. As the group size increases, having more than one coach can enhance the process for all involved.

Ethical delivery and interpretation of group-level assessments include various components:

- A key element is that at least one coach needs to be certified in and experienced with the assessment tool being used.

- Providing individual feedback before offering group feedback and initiating team-development exercises will increase the success of the intervention. From an ethical perspective, the individual feedback session allows the coach time to address individual issues or concerns privately and obtain agreement from individuals to share group data.

- The most effective team interventions that include assessments contain individual coaching elements, informal sharing among team members, and an agreed-upon plan for team sharing. Ethical practice means having a plan for these elements before undertaking this type of coaching engagement. For example, a plan might include individual feedback sessions for all participants, group interpretation of the assessment tool, and structured group exercises around the tool. You might provide follow-up activities for the team, individual group members, or both.

Another type of group-assessment process is that in which a collection of individuals use the same assessment tool(s) and participate in structured exercises around the tool(s). Coaching for career-exploration issues often utilizes a group format, so that participants can learn from each other while they follow a structured process led by the coach. The focus is on each individual's data, rather than on group dynamics. Individual group members may choose to share with other group members, but doing so is generally not an expectation.

A key to ethical practice is specifying and agreeing upon the process and members' expectations in advance.

Individual Assessments

Individual-level assessments are used in a variety of settings, so, as a coach, understanding the range of relevant assessment tools can be quite helpful. You might never choose to administer an assessment tool, but your clients most likely will have used one somewhere and will have stories about that tool or the process. Whatever clients respond to in the assessment tool or process is information for the coaching relationship.

Clients sometimes bring in assessment-tool results from another setting. Even if you are not familiar with the particular assessment tool, you can ask the client about what was learned from the assessment tool, the feedback process, and the reasons for bringing in the assessment tool at this time. The focus stays on helping the client gain insights by linking previous learning with new experiences. You can generally find some information about the assessment tool on the Web after the session.

Combination approaches might be used when an organization is implementing a new leadership-development effort. Organizational and group assessments are used to identify critical leadership competencies for the organization. Individual assessment packages, with feedback and individual follow-up coaching, are provided for leaders throughout the organization. Group or team assessments might also be incorporated.

The Feedback Plan

Whenever you use an assessment tool, have a plan for feedback. The feedback session (coaching process) is the most critical part of the assessment process, and is where the real learning occurs. Your feedback should be tied to desired objectives for both the client and the process, and be relevant to the context. Additionally, providing practical, behavioral examples rather than relying on technical jargon will make the results more meaningful and useful. Remember to ask what fits and does not fit with clients' perceptions, and be prepared to listen to the meaning clients make from the results. A strengths-based approach to feedback is most consistent with the coaching model. Providing appropriate feedback about an assessment tool is an art that can be learned and that generally improves with practice.

Types of Assessment Tools

The development of assessment tools is growing at a pace similar to the coaching profession itself, with new tools coming out regularly. A comprehensive overview of all assessment tools on the market is beyond the scope of this chapter, so we will focus on some assessment tools that coaches see with some frequency today. We will explore personal-style, emotional-intelligence, career, multirater, and leadership-development assessment tools and practices. We have chosen a few assessment tools for illustrative purposes. The inclusion of these instruments is not a formal endorsement of any certain instrument, nor is the exclusion of any instrument meant to downplay its effectiveness.

Personal-Style and Personality Assessment Tools

Tools that explore various personal-style dimensions are fairly common. These assessment tools are used in the workplace, with community groups, in classes, and in coaching sessions. These assessments generally are self-report measures in which individuals complete a paper-and-pencil questionnaire or use a computer to respond to questions. The test report is a summary of a person's responses to the questions, plotted along various dimensions.

Personality tests are more rigorous, in-depth assessments that are administered and interpreted by professionals with training in assessment processes. Because personality tests go into more depth and are often used for distinct purposes, they require specialized training and skill.

Many personal-style assessment tools are on the market, and coaches will hear about them from their clients. We will focus our discussion primarily on self-report personal-style instruments. Feedback with these instruments focuses on what each dimension of the assessment means and how persons score on each dimension. Higher scores in a dimension category usually mean stronger preferences in that dimension, while lower scores mean less preference differentiation in the dimension. An assessment instrument may examine one or several different dimensions. Because these are self-report measures, they are contingent upon respondents' self-awareness and willingness to respond in an open and honest manner. As coach, you might get some information about your clients' preferences from these results; you will definitely get information about your clients' perceptions of the assessment results.

Personal-preference tools are designed to increase self-awareness and awareness of alternate preferences. Many people do not consciously think about how their personal preferences affect their behavior; hence, increasing their awareness of such factors may have a positive impact on them in terms of behavior change. People also have a natural tendency to not really consider that other people may have some very different preferences from their own. Increased awareness of personal preferences and alternate preferences that others have can reduce conflict and enhance communication.

> A key ethical issue here is the importance of not becoming overly focused on the labels, categories, or types described in assessment tools. If people feel that they are being labeled, typed, or categorized, they will respond negatively to the assessment process, which is harmful to them as clients as well as to the overall process. The role of the coach is to facilitate in clients increased awareness of self and others, and to avoid any labeling. If a client complains about labeling that occurred from an assessment elsewhere, the coach, after responding to the client's frustration about being labeled, can help that client look for potential learning from the assessment process. Sometimes, a personal-style assessment is quite accurate, but the person cannot relate to the information because of a reaction to labeling or to the perceptions of labeling.

Some frequently used personal-style instruments include Enneagram, Myers-Briggs Type Indicator (MBTI), DISC, Birkman, FIRO-B, Strength Deployment Inventory, Sixteen Personality Factor, Edwards Personal Preference Schedule, Insight Inventory, California Personality Inventory, Thomas-Killman Conflict Profile, and Conflict Dynamics Profile. These instruments require varying degrees of graduate-level training, or successful completion of a several-day certification program, or both.

To use assessment tools effectively, proper training is essential. Most coaches have heard stories about good assessment tools used improperly by well-meaning individuals who are not adequately trained in assessment processes. As already emphasized, it is important to maintain ethical standards for the coaching profession throughout the assessment process.

> If a coach is not qualified or trained to deliver a certain type of assessment, the coach should make the ethical choice to subcontract the assessment to someone who is qualified and certified in the use of the instrument.

Because the Myers-Briggs Type Indicator (MBTI) is a fairly well-known self-report assessment tool that has been around for many years, we will examine its use a little more closely as it relates to coaching practice. The MBTI measures individual preferences along four dimensions that have an impact upon natural responses in different situations. The *introversion-extroversion scale* examines whether a person prefers to re-charge personal energy by spending time alone or with other people. The *sensing-intuitive scale* gets at preferences for dealing with facts or with possibilities. The *thinking-feeling scale* assesses one's primary filter for making decisions—logic or personal values. The *judging-perceiving scale* focuses on preferences for decision and closure versus keeping things flexible and open. There are no right or wrong answers, and people may change on some dimensions over time. These are all preferences, not absolute behavior measures. For example, having a preference for introversion does not mean one is a recluse, lacking in interpersonal skill; it simply indicates a preference for having some alone time to energize oneself. Distinctions can be made for each of the other dimensions, as well. This tool illustrates some general preferences among individuals, and how these preferences affect people in their daily lives.

> Remember, the ethical coach does not use the information to label or put people into definitive, exclusionary categories or boxes.

Most coaches, if they are so inclined, can become certified through several different organizations to use the MBTI. The basic certification course is several days long and culminates in an exam to ensure that users adequately understand the instrument. Beyond the basic certification course are numerous other courses focused on coaching, career development, team building, relationship enhancement, and linkages with other assessment tools. Several books about using the Myers–Briggs Type Indicator in practice are available, just as there are books for many of the other personal-style assessments (Kroeger & Thuesen, 1988, 1992). The actual requirements for each assessment tool vary, so you will need to explore the options and requirements if and when you decide to seek certification in a particular assessment tool.

Career-Assessment Tools

Assessment tools are frequently used in career coaching. The objective is to provide individuals a wide range of information to aid in career decision making. A package may include interest assessments, ability or aptitude testing, skill ratings, and personality or personal-style inventories. For interest assessment, the Strong Interest Inventory, the Self-Directed Search, and computer programs such as *SIGI* and *Discover* have been in use for many years. These tools rely on theories of career choice put forth by John Holland and Donald Super, which assert that people will most likely be happiest and successful in careers consistent with certain interest and personality patterns. These assessments include career clusters that focus on working with ideas, things, and people. Skill-card sorts and surveys such as the Campbell

Interest and Skill Survey help people identify learned skills. Personal-style preference-assessment tools examine personality dimensions from the job- or work-environment perspective. These tools are self-report instruments and depend on how clients respond to the questions. Assessments might include extensive computerized reports, as in the Strong Interest Inventory, or they might be self-scored paper-and-pencil instruments.

> A key ethical issue related to the use of these kinds of assessments is that a career inventory is only one piece of information—its results should not be considered the final answer.

Another category of career-assessment tools is the *ability assessment*, which is a timed instrument whose results are compared with standardized scores to provide information about natural, inborn talents. The Highlands Ability Battery, for example, measures many natural abilities, including driving abilities and learning channels, to help people select careers in which they will be successful and satisfied. McDonald and Hutcheson (1997, 2000) assert that one must consider eight critical factors for effective career decision making. These factors include abilities, skills, interests, values, personality aspects, family influences, life goals, and the career-development cycle. The career-development cycle builds upon the work of developmental psychology for adults and is described by Hudson (1999) in *The Adult Years and the Handbook of Coaching*. People have different developmental needs and corresponding career issues throughout life. For instance, there are periods of building and stability, and periods of change and reconstruction.

> To maintain ethical practices in using career- and ability-assessment tools, it is a good idea to share

155

this developmental process with clients, so they can view career exploration and career change as the norm.

Career assessment and coaching can be a rather extensive process. Qualified coaches may administer and interpret various assessment tools. Another option is for you as the coach to work with someone else who does the assessment and feedback session, and then you provide the important follow-up coaching to help clients integrate the information, search out alternatives, and carry through on detailed action plans. Without follow-up coaching, clients may jump to quick and incomplete decisions and never fully make use of the assessment information provided. Or they may arrive at some inaccurate conclusions.

Your ethical practice ensures that clients understand the results of the assessments. As the coach, you guide individuals and groups through the longer-term processes that career-exploration work often requires.

Emotional-Intelligence Assessment Tools

Goleman (1998a, 1998b) and Robins (2002) suggest that the key factors separating exceptional leaders from average performers are related to emotional intelligence. Emotional intelligence turns out to be more important than IQ and technical skills for success among jobs at all levels, and has great applicability for coaching (Megerian & Megerian, 1999).

Goleman (1998a, 1998b) describes four components of emotional intelligence that can be assessed with the Emotional Competency Inventory (ECI): self-awareness, self-management, social awareness, and relationship management. Goleman contends that self-awareness is the foundation for enhancing leadership and personal development, and that self-awareness is essential to learn self-regulation strategies, have empathy, read social situations, and effectively manage relationships. There are several versions of the ECI—paper and pencil, computerized, self-report only, and multirater. Assessment of emotional intelligence has become increasingly popular, and a variety of other assessment tools in addition to the ECI are available to assess dimensions of emotional intelligence (Garman, 2002).

Goleman's (2000) research has demonstrated a link between emotional intelligence, leadership styles, and organizational culture. As measured in the Leadership Style Inventory, six leadership styles include coercive, authoritative, affiliative, democratic, pace setting, and coaching. The most effective leaders use several of these styles interchangeably rather than one style exclusively. Leadership styles have an impact on elements of organizational culture, which in turn affect employee performance and the bottom line. The behavior of leaders sets the tone for the culture of an entire organization (Schein, 1992). The Organizational Culture Survey identifies specific elements of culture. By assessing leader emotional intelligence and leadership style(s), one can use the results to modify leadership to improve effectiveness and affect organizational culture. The emotional-competence model is based on a behavioral approach to change, so you as a coach can help clients increase their self-awareness as they develop empathy, social skills, and self-management capabilities; and self-awareness is an important foundation for ethical behavior.

Multirater Assessments

The use of multirater assessments, sometimes referred to as *360-degree feedback*, is rapidly growing in organizations. This method is used to obtain information about how leaders' behaviors are viewed by those above them, by those below them, by their peers and colleagues, and by themselves. Inconsistency across raters is generally a focus in feed-back and follow-up coaching.

Having top management identify the most important leadership competencies for the organization provides an important frame of reference for multirater assessments because assessment tools need to be consistent with organizational culture and desired leadership com-petencies (Chappelow, 1998). Although certain behaviors are essen-tial for all effective leaders, some leadership behaviors are unique to certain industries, roles, and cultures. The behaviors and competen-cies that contribute to success in one setting may jeopardize success in other settings—this is particularly true for leaders as they move up through different *levels* of leadership (Charan, Drotter, & Noel, 2001). Therefore, it is very important to link leadership competen-cies and behaviors with clients' industry and organizational context.

Critical to the multirater assessment process are the decisions about how to use the assessment data: with whom it will be shared, who is to be included in the data-collection process, and how the results will be given to the individual who was evaluated. As coach, you must be keenly aware of ethical issues in this process. Most experts recommend that you share the assessment results only with the individual being rated (Chappelow, 1998). Getting everyone's agreement to this arrangement from the start encourages the raters to be candid in their assessments and creates an atmosphere for growth and development.

If the results are to be shared with others in the organization, as coach, you may have additional ethical issues to consider. For exam-ple, an organization may want information about assessment results to facilitate the development of individual leaders. The individual leaders can provide a summary of assessment data to the organization or include selected parts in a development plan. Discussion of multi-rater feedback data can enhance relationships between and among leaders and their bosses, peers, and subordinates. This option gives leaders an opportunity to discuss their performance and developmental needs with those who regularly experience their behavior and its consequences. These people can then support the leaders in implementing their respective development plans. As coach, you might be asked to help draft a summary of the assessment data for the organization, create a development plan, and prepare for a conversation with raters.

> Clarification of the process, roles, and expectations is important at the outset of the coaching engagement.

Interpreting multirater assessment data in a coaching feedback session is a very important part of the process (Fleenor & Prince, 1997). Assessment results need to be tied to the work context and the competencies required within the organization. Giving assessment-tool results with minimal interpretive data is not an effective way to use multirater data, yet it happens. If the feedback process is handled poorly, recipients may do any or all of the following: focus exclusively on negative parts of the assessment, dismiss the results as invalid, attempt to find out who said what about them, feel angry, or become less productive.

> A key ethical issue here is that your role as coach is to help individuals understand the feedback provided and put that feedback to constructive use. To overlook this part of the process is harmful to the client(s).

Numerous multirater feedback instruments are on the market today, and choosing an appropriate multirater leadership–assessment tool is no easy task. Some comprehensive instruments that have a strong research base include Leadership Effectiveness Analysis, by Management Research Group; Benchmarks, from Center for Creative Leadership; and Profiler, by Personnel Decisions International. These assessments are restricted-access instruments that are sold only to qualified users with appropriate education and successful completion of a certification program. If you need a high-quality multirater leadership assessment for your coaching practice, and you are not qualified to administer it, we encourage you to contract someone qualified to complete the assessment and feedback process. Then you can help the client make the best use of the data in the ongoing coaching relationship.

As a coach, you may become trained in and certified to use some multirater assessment tools that link theoretical models and leadership-development programs. Covey (1989, 1990) has an assessment instrument to complement his theory of principled leadership. Bass (1985, 1990, 1995; Fields & Herold, 1997) translated his ideas on transactional and transformational leadership into a leadership questionnaire. Blanchard's (1998) situational-leadership model focuses on flexibility in leadership behavior to match specific situations. Kouzes and Posner (1995) designed the Leadership Practices Inventory (LPI) after they had interviewed hundreds of employees over two decades to determine what they wanted in a leader. The traits that consistently received high ratings were honesty, competence, forward-looking viewpoint, inspiration, and credibility. Their research (1987, 1993, 1995) led them to articulate in *The Leadership Challenge* five key themes that define effective leadership:

- Challenging the process
- Inspiring a shared vision
- Enabling others to act

- Modeling behaviors
- Encouraging the heart

In *Credibility: How Leaders Gain and Lose It, Why People Demand It* (1993), the authors elaborate on themes that foster credibility, the essential component of leadership. Posner and Kouzes (1994) have also extended their work on leadership to individual contributors.

Leadership-Development Practices

A variety of assessment tools are used in leadership-development efforts. The essential components usually depend on the leadership theory and model an organization espouses (Graham & Robinson, 2002). There are many theories of leadership development, and coaches wishing to work with leaders are encouraged to become knowledgeable of the theories and models in practice. Most leadership-development programs use a combination of multirater assessments, self-assessments, feedback, coaching, mentoring, challenge assignments, and skill training related to emotional-intelligence competencies (McCauley, Moxley, & Van Velsor, 1998; Garman, 2002). Combined approaches are generally more effective than a single-strategy approach (Guthrie & Kelly-Radford, 1998).

Assessment tools can provide leaders some much-needed feedback. As people progress in organizational-leadership positions, obtaining honest feedback becomes increasingly difficult. Saporito (1996) contends that senior executives tend to become isolated from real-time, unvarnished feedback about the impact of their individual leadership. Subordinates often feel uncomfortable providing candid feedback to their superiors, yet people need candid and constructive information about how they affect others and how they can improve (Chappelow, 1998; Kirkland & Manoogian, 1998). If coaches handle assessment tools with competence and have other ethical practices in place, they can provide a valuable service by helping leaders obtain and use feedback effectively. Self-assessment tools used in conjunction with multirater assessment tools allow leaders and their coaches to compare self-assessment data against the impressions of others. Feedback from others can be viewed as threatening, but such feedback is often the most highly valued aspect of the leadership-development program (Guthrie & Kelly-Radford, 1998). With effective feedback and follow-up coaching, assessment tools can create a readiness to learn on the part of the leaders.

Organizations might use individual assessment tools as a part of the screening and selection process for leadership positions, for developing high-potential employees, and for promoting the development of current leaders (Garman, 2002). They might also use assessment tools to help leaders who are struggling, or at risk of derailing, to provide insight into some personal factors that affect the leaders' work.

Such a leadership-assessment package generally includes a multirater leadership survey, a personality inventory or style-preference instrument, an ability or aptitude assessment, and a skill rating. Personality assessments provide insight into one's overall personality dimensions, while other instruments focus on specific personal factors such as motivation and emotional competence. Aptitude and skill assessments can enhance the match between job and skill sets. Ability batteries identify specific abilities and combinations as they relate to success and satisfaction in work roles. Assessment of general cognitive ability may be part of the selection process for management positions.

A professional trained in assessment processes may conduct a pre-assessment interview and interpret the data in a feedback session. After an extensive feedback session, a client may feel overwhelmed with information, and have a tendency to focus on what is not positive. Executive coaches help leaders integrate the information into the context of the organization, their current leadership role, and targeted future leadership positions (Hawkins & Petty, 2000). The coaches continue working with leaders to create and implement their development plans.

Using assessments as a foundation for individual development planning with follow-up coaching is a significant trend in organizations' leadership-development programs (Giber, Carter, & Goldsmith, 2000). An individual development plan helps integrate new information into a useable format, and creates an appropriate course for development. Without a plan, leadership-development activities can become random events that may or may not promote leadership development. Setting a particular course and checking progress allows the leader to develop over time. Most people can successfully change one or two behaviors at a time, so, as a coach, you should consider this information when you are creating individual development plans (Waagan, 2001). You can help leaders think strategically about their behavior-change agenda and provide ongoing support as the leaders pursue their development plans.

This chapter has described a variety of assessment tools coaches use. This sample by no means covers the full range of choices on the market today, and we have not mentioned many high-quality assessment tools. Being familiar with these tools and their processes is advantageous to you, the professional coach, and you need to be clear about your limits of knowledge and professional expertise of assessment tools. You must also work to stay up to date on new developments in the field.

Selection of Quality Assessment Tools

If you are going to use assessment tools, it is important to use those of high quality and to understand their properties. Anastasi (1982) is a well-known expert on psychological testing. Her book *Psychological*

Testing has been printed in numerous editions and represents a staple in many graduate courses on the subject. Here we review a few of Anastasi's critical concepts as they relate to the professional practice of assessment.

A psychological test is an objective and standardized measure of a sample of behavior. *Standardization* implies uniformity of procedure in administering and scoring the test. If the scores obtained by different persons are to be comparable, testing conditions need to be the same for all. Standardization is a major ethical issue. *Reliability* is the consistency of scores obtained by the same person when retested with the identical test or an equivalent form. The most important question to ask about any psychological test concerns *validity*, or the degree to which the test actually measures what it purports to measure. Validity is another important ethical issue. Validity provides a direct check on how well the test fulfills its function. In the process of standardizing a test, it is administered to a large, representative sample of the types of persons for whom it is designed. It is also important to know about the *norm group* upon which the instrument was standardized, and one also needs to consider gender and cultural differences when interpreting an individual's test results compared to a norm group. A client may ask about the norm, or comparison group upon which the instrument is based, as well as issues related to reliability and validity.

The test manual should provide the essential information for administering, scoring, and evaluating an instrument. The manual should contain detailed instructions, scoring information, norms, and data on reliability and validity. Therefore, reading the assessment manual is important because it provides essential information about the tool.

> Ethical practice means that you as the coach will
> evaluate the assessment tool before you choose it

for your specific purposes, and that you will choose to use the tool only because it fits the needs of your clientele.

Qualifications to Use Instruments

Professional coaches who have graduate training in psychology, counseling, or a related field have access to several exclusive assessment instruments that are not available for purchase by the general public (Auerbach, 2001). Psychologists receive specialized training in test administration, interpretation, and feedback on numerous assessment tools. These meta-skills they have learned during graduate training enable psychologists to select and effectively use a full range of assessment tools (APA, 2004). Coaches, however, may also have other, additional organizational professional guidelines to consider when they are using assessment tools.

As mentioned previously, coaches can become certified to use a range of assessment tools, depending on their professional background, educational training, and interests. The certification process provides extensive information about the assessment tools and how to use them effectively. It also enables the coach to purchase assessment materials for use. Some companies post certified users on their websites, so coaches can choose to be listed, or they can find someone who is certified to use an instrument. The process of certification can be expensive in terms of time commitment and dollar costs, so you should be certain you want to be certified in a particular assessment tool before you pursue the process.

Ethical practice dictates that, as a coach, you should:

- Not administer an assessment tool you are not qualified and certified to use.
- Purchase assessment tools from a testing company or individual

who owns the tool. Most instruments are considered intellectual property and are copyrighted, so you should not copy an instrument and use it.

- Be cognizant of presenting services you are qualified to provide, and refrain from attempting to provide a service you are not certified or qualified to offer.

Observing these guidelines is ethical practice at its best.

General Professional Practice Issues—A Recap

As an ethical practitioner

- Know your limits. Subcontracting another coach or other qualified professional for one assessment tool or an entire package is a way to incorporate assessment tools into your coaching practice. You can provide follow-up coaching for individuals after they complete assessment-feedback processes. If you are an executive coach, you are likely to be contracted often to work with leaders for development planning and execution. Consider developing niches and areas of expertise. Sometimes coaches become certified in tools specific to their areas of expertise.

- Be wary of simplifying something so much that clients fear being labeled or categorized by assessment tools.

- Also be aware of cultural differences in response to assessment tools. Some assessment tools are available in several languages and have norm groups for different cultures; others do not. Accommodating cultural differences as you use assessment tools is an important ethical issue you must not overlook.

- Consider confidentiality when using assessment tools. From the beginning of the coaching engagement, it is important to consider and reach agreement about who owns the assessment results. This can become a tricky issue when organizations contract the coach. For the coaching and assessment process to have integrity, all parties need to know the parameters regarding who gets to know what.

Conclusion

Assessments can be a valuable tool in a coaching engagement. Assessments can increase self-awareness and provide information to enhance relationships. In leadership development, assessments are often the foundation for development planning and executive coaching. Ethical practice means that coaches know their limitations as evaluators. They know what tool is appropriate for which situation, and, if need be, they obtain another professional to administer the assessment and interpret the results. Last, but surely not least, coaches clearly define the boundaries around the use of the information they gain through the assessment process.

Case Study

Coach A has been coaching Leader B, who recently moved to a new position. The move from individual contributor to manager of frontline supervisors, technical staff, analysts, and support staff has been a challenge for Leader B. He describes a sense of something missing, that things do not get done on time, and a feeling of tension among people in the department.

Staff Member C comes to talk with Leader B, excited about an assessment tool called Myers-Briggs Type Indicator (MBTI) that she used as part of her women's group at church. The staff member described how the MBTI helped her understand why

(Continued)

167

she and her sister had a series of ongoing conflicts. She says, "I like to have things neat, orderly, and planned well in advance. I am also very vocal about it. For my sister, everything is last minute, and she never tells us anything. We were sitting next to each other in the group when we got our assessment results, and we looked at each other with huge smiles on our faces. The more the facilitator talked about the different characteristics, the more we smiled. We both got it. Do you think we could use the MBTI for the whole department?" Leader B says he will think about it.

During the next coaching session, Leader B brings up Staff Member C's request with his coach. Coach A is familiar with the MBTI, but has never given the instrument and is not certified to use it. Coach A probes Leader B about the purpose, goals, and potential outcomes of a group session with the MBTI. Coach A suggests that Leader B check out the interests of the rest of the staff in using the assessment tool.

Between sessions, Coach A contacts Coach D, who did a presentation at the local International Coach Federation meeting a few months ago on the MBTI, to discuss the use of the instrument in coaching, and Coach D's interest and availability to work with him and the department of 15 people. Coach D says she is interested and could work with Coach A on the project.

At the next staff meeting, Leader B brings up Staff Member C's suggestion to the entire group. He invites her to share her experience. Some staff members seem excited, and a few seem reticent to engage in the process. The reticent ones want to know exactly what they would have to do. The consensus is to get more information about the assessment tool and group activity before they proceed.

Questions

1. Has Coach A acted responsibly and ethically with his client?
2. What obligations does Coach A have to Coach D?

3. Should Coach A take the MBTI before having his client and staff take it?
4. What is the next step in this process?
5. If they proceed with this project, what safeguards must Coach A put into place?
6. What would you do if you were Coach A?

REFERENCES

American Psychological Association Board of Educational Affairs (2004). *APA guidelines for education and training at the doctoral and post-doctoral level in consulting psychology/organizational consulting psychology.* Washington, D.C.: APA.

Anastasi, A. (1982). *Psychological testing.* New York: MacMillan Publishing.

Auerbach, J.E. (2001). *Personal and executive coaching.* Ventura, California: Executive College Press.

Bass, B.M. (1985). *Leadership and performance beyond expectations.* New York: Free Press.

———— (1990). From transactional to transformational leadership: Learning to share vision. *Organizational Dynamics 19*(1), 19–31.

———— (1995). Comment: Transformational leadership. *Journal of Management Inquiry 4*, 293–297.

Blanchard, K. (1998). *Insights on leadership.* In L.C. Spears (Ed.), *Servant leadership revisited* (pp. 21–28). New York: Wiley & Sons.

Chappelow, C.T. (1998). *The Center for Creative Leadership handbook of leadership development.* In C.D. McCauley, R.S. Moxley, & E. Van Velsor (Eds.), *360-degree feedback* (pp. 29–65). San Francisco: Jossey Bass.

Charan, R., Drotter, S., & Noel, J. (2001) *The leadership pipeline.* San Francisco: Jossey Bass.

Covey, S. (1989). *The seven habits of highly effective people.* New York: Fireside.

———— (1990). *Principle-centered leadership.* New York: Fireside.

Deeprose, D. (1995). *The team coach.* New York: The American Management Association.

Fields, D., & Harold, D. (1997). Using the leadership practices inventory to measure transformational and transactional leadership. *Educational & Psychological Measurement 57,* 569–579.

Fleenor, J.W., & Prince, J.M. (1997). *Using 360-degree feedback in organizations.* Greensboro, NC: Center for Creative Leadership.

Garman, A.N. (2002) Assessing candidates for leadership positions. In R. L. Lowman (Ed.), *Handbook of organizational consulting psychology* (pp. 185–211). San Francisco: Jossey Bass.

Giber, D., Carter, L., & Goldsmith, M. (Eds.) (2000). *Linkage Inc.'s best practices in leadership development handbook.* San Francisco: Jossey Bass.

Goleman, D. (1998a). Leadership that gets results. *Harvard Business Review 76*(2), 78–90.

———— (1998b). *Working with emotional intelligence.* New York: Bantam.

———— (2000). What makes a leader? *Harvard Business Review 78*(1), 93–102.

Graham, S., & Robinson, D. (2002). Leadership development in organizational consulting. In R.L. Lowman (Ed.), *Handbook of organizational consulting psychology* (pp. 370–395). San Francisco: Jossey Bass.

Guthrie, V.A., & Kelly-Radford, L. (1998). Feedback-intensive programs. In C.D. McCauley, R.S. Moxley, & E. Van Velsor (Eds.),

The Center for Creative Leadership handbook of leadership development (pp. 66–105). San Francisco: Jossey Bass.

Hawkins, B., & Petty, T. (2000). *Coaching for leadership.* In M. Goldsmith, L. Lyons, & A. Freas (Eds.), *Coaching for organizational change* (pp. 307–315). San Francisco: Jossey Bass.

Hudson, F.M. (1999). *The adult years: Mastering the art of self-renewal.* San Francisco: Jossey Bass.

——— (1999). *Handbook of coaching.* San Francisco: Jossey Bass.

Kirkland, K., & Manoogian, S. (1998). *Ongoing feedback: How to get it, how to use it.* Greensboro, NC: Center for Creative Leadership.

Kouzes, J., & Posner, B. (1987). *The leadership challenge.* San Francisco: Jossey Bass.

——— (1993). *Credibility: How leaders gain and lose it, why people demand it.* San Francisco: Jossey Bass.

——— (1995). *The leadership challenge: How to keep getting extraordinary things done in organizations.* San Francisco: Jossey Bass.

Kroeger, O., & Thuesen, J. (1988). *Type talk: The sixteen personality types that determine how we live, love, and work.* New York: Dell Publishing.

——— (1992). *Type talk at work.* New York: Dell Publishing.

McCauley, C., Moxley, R., & Van Velsor, E. (1998). *Handbook of leadership development.* San Francisco: Jossey Bass.

McDonald, B.D., & Hutcheson, D. (1997). *The lemming conspiracy.* Marietta, Georgia: Longstreet Press.

——— (2000). *Don't waste your talent.* Marietta, Georgia: Longstreet Press.

Megerian, J., & Megerian, L. (1999). Understanding leader emotional intelligence and performance. *Group & Organization Management 24,* 367–393.

Posner, B., & Kouzes, J. (1994). An extension of the Leadership Practices Inventory to individual contributors. *Educational & Psychological Measurement 54,* 959–966.

Robins, S. (2002). A consultant's guide to understanding and promoting emotional intelligence in the workplace. In R.L. Lowman (Ed.), *Handbook of organizational consulting psychology* (pp. 159–184). San Francisco: Jossey Bass.

Saporito, T. J. (1996). Business linked executive development: Coaching senior executives. *Consulting Psychology Journal: Practice and Research 48,* 96–103.

Schein, E. (1992). *Organizational culture and leadership.* San Francisco: Jossey Bass.

Waagan, A.J. (2001). Individual development plans for leaders. *ASTD Performance in Practice,* 2–3.

8

Legal Issues and Solutions for Coaches

**William H. Lindberg and
Andrew R. Desmond**

Objectives

This chapter introduces the legal issues that affect your coaching practice. A comprehensive "Law of Coaching" could be a multivolume work, so please think of this chapter as an *introduction* to the breadth and variety of legal issues you face in starting and operating your coaching practice. These issues include, but are certainly not limited to:

- The choice of structure for your business entity and relevant tax considerations

- Naming your business legally and ethically

- Contracting with your clients legally and ethically

- Regulatory issues that affect coaching (and boundary issues with related fields such as psychotherapy, career counseling, marriage and family therapy, etc.)

- Intellectual property issues, such as copyright and trademark laws

- Insurance requirements for your coaching practice

- Emerging legal issues in the field of coaching

Pre-Chapter Self-Assessment Test

1. Under current U.S. copyright law, copyright attaches the moment an original work is created; a notice of copyright is helpful but not mandatory to protect one's creative work.

   a. True　　　　b. False

2. A coach can almost always insulate herself from being sued for negligence by a well-crafted engagement letter.

   a. True　　　　b. False

3. It is fully legal to reproduce a *New Yorker* cartoon or a Gary Larson *Far Side* cartoon in a presentation as long as I identify and attribute the cartoon to its source.

   a. True　　　　b. False

4. Because the coaching process can be therapeutic and cathartic to clients, it is generally advisable to frame my engagement letter in terms of the psychological benefits that can be derived from the coaching process.

   a. True　　　　b. False

5. Because there is really no harm that can come from casting my credentials in the most positive light, it is acceptable and common practice to slightly exaggerate my experience in a

particular area of coaching, especially when I have taken a three-day seminar.

a. True   b. False

6. With the client's permission, it is acceptable for me to publicly disclose the content of a coach–client conversation.

a. True   b. False

7. Because the content of a coaching conversation can cover very private and intimate subject matter, most state and federal courts have adopted a coach–client privilege that protects the content of coaching conversations from the discovery process in litigation.

a. True   b. False

8. When one is selecting the form of a business, a partnership is desirable because it offers limited liability for the partners.

a. True   b. False

9. The Anglo–American legal system uses a principle based on the notion that precedents should generally be followed.

a. True   b. False

10. The laws that most directly affect coaching are generally federal laws, and agencies such as the Federal Trade Commission typically issue business licenses to coaches.

a. True   b. False

11. States generally recognize credentials of coaches who graduate from coaching schools accredited by the International Coach Federation as a basic equivalent of licensure.

a. True   b. False

Introduction

> *"In civilized life, law floats on a sea of ethics. Each is indispensable to civilization. Without law, we should be at the mercy of the least scrupulous; without ethics, law could not exist."*
>
> —Earl Warren

As Earl Warren noted, the relationship between law and ethics is inextricable. The specific requirements of laws and regulations frequently serve to implement the more general concepts and ethical principles that underlie legal rules. Because of the limitations of language, even the most carefully conceived legal rule is susceptible to unavoidable ambiguity.

In essence, "Law is the intersection of language and power. Lawyers use words to persuade, to justify, and to govern" (Shapiro, 1993). Coaching, in contrast, dwells in the domain of personal growth, eliciting clarity and generating action. In coaching, client interactions frequently involve language and intense emotion, but the manner in which these interactions occur varies dramatically. Abraham Lincoln noted that a lawyer's time and advice are his stock in trade. Lawyers give advice based on their understanding of a given set of facts, and based on the knowledge of laws that a judge would apply if the matter was reviewed in court. That approach is anathema to coaching.

Coaching is not giving advice. It is not about fixing things or solving problems. Coaching is establishing a vital relationship over a period of time with clients who are searching for the clarity and skills needed for making changes in their lives and human systems (couples, family, work, communities) in the near future.

The product of coaching comes from the bond between coach and client. . . . Coaching works to connect two dimensions of a client: the inner being or self and some outer action(s) or performance. (Hudson, 1999)

The law is an ancient profession, but coaching, as we know it today, is a newly emergent field. For this reason, the intersection of law and coaching is still evolving and taking shape. Lawyers dwell in the domain of rules, regulations, and precedent. The Anglo-American common law is founded on a principle known as *stare decisis et non quieta movere,* which means "to stand by things decided, and not to disturb settled points." It is useful to remember this maxim because coaching, as a field, is still in its infancy. Therefore, very few direct legal precedents are available for lawyers who provide guidance to coaches. Through analogy, statutes, and court cases that affect closely related fields, the contours and boundaries of coaching are beginning to emerge with more clarity. As coaching evolves, as the number of coaches proliferates, and as the economic impact of coaching grows, heightened attention will be given to the legal aspects of coaching because boundary questions with other fields will intensify.

The answer to each legal question depends on the local, state, and national laws in effect where you coach; therefore, the matters covered in this chapter provide only general guidance. You will need specific legal advice from an attorney near you, some of it general in nature, and some of it highly specialized. The law, much like modern medicine, is divided into specialty disciplines. For example, a good small-business lawyer can advise you in start-up and general matters, just as your family practitioner can advise you on your basic health needs. However, when you run into situations that call for specialized legal counsel, your small-business generalist (like your family doctor) can help you select a specialized attorney (see "At What Point Should I Hire an Attorney for My Coaching Practice?" later in the chapter).

179

Coaching is still a relatively new field, but specialized niches have emerged (Hudson, 1999; Williams, 2002, pp. 9–22). The range of practice spans from working in the executive suite of a company's CEO to providing personal coaching to individuals on issues of lifestyle balance and family matters. Nevertheless, some legal aspects in the field of coaching tend to apply to many types of coaching practice.

As a practitioner, you may be tempted to view the red tape of coaching practice as administrivia and set legal formalities aside until they scream for attention. To do so is at your peril! We encourage you to carefully consider the issues this chapter raises and be sure to pay attention to them either personally or through a team of advisors. We will provide general guidance and practical tools, such as checklists, forms, and resources for further guidance in technical areas. Please note: Use this chapter as background and not as a substitute for local legal advice.

The goal of this chapter is to focus on general legal issues that will arise in virtually every coaching practice. We also provide practical solutions that allow you to step over the initial hurdles as a professional coach in establishing your enterprise. A list of the issues addressed include:

- Professional liability
- Steps to selecting a legal name for the coaching practice
- Licensure and coaching
- Formal contracts with clients
- Hiring an attorney
- Intellectual property
- Insurance
- Best practices

Do I Need to Incorporate My Coaching Practice?

*"They (corporations) cannot commit treason, nor be out-
lawed, nor excommunicate, for they have no souls."*

—Sir Edward Coke, English Jurist Case of
Sutton's Hospital

In American, as well as English, jurisprudence, corporations enjoy
perpetual existence. If only we coaches, individually, were so lucky!
Most coaching practices need not incorporate. There are several
cheaper alternatives to incorporating, and each of them imposes
fewer restrictions than corporations do. Most individual coaches
operate by default as a sole proprietorship, or they choose to register
as a limited liability company. In this section, we help you probe the
specific nature of your coaching practice through a series of simple
questions. This process will help you identify the best business structure for your situation. You can change from one business structure
to another as your practice evolves, but you will incur costs and
headaches doing so. Therefore, choose a business entity at the outset
that will serve your immediate needs as well as your foreseeable needs
for the next one to three years.

Business Structures and Other Means of Limiting Coaching Liability

You can operate a professional coaching practice using any business
structure that your state's law recognizes. Most states recognize four
basic business structures, or entities: *sole proprietorship, partnership, limited liability company,* and *corporation.*

If you choose to operate as a corporation under state law, you
have a further choice to make: whether to have the corporation pay

its federal taxes as an entity (a Subchapter C Corporation), or to avoid double taxation by having individual owners of the corporation pay their pro rata share of the corporation's taxes via their individual tax returns (a so-called Subchapter S Corporation).

For several reasons, states sanction several different legal structures for operating a profit-making enterprise. The primary reason is to separate business obligations from personal ones. Another reason is to give business customers recourse against the business, while protecting the pocketbooks of the individuals who operate the business. Not all businesses are alike, so different legal structures have emerged to fit the nature of the enterprise.

Consider this: If limited liability business structures did not exist, wronged customers would have their lawyers file suit against every conceivable individual who may have contributed to a bad business practice or decision. That practice would result in extraordinary costs of doing business, and it would stifle entrepreneurship. Those who operate businesses for profit need limitations on personal liability in order to continue providing goods and services to the public without the specter of personal financial disaster. A coach, like other service providers, should feel secure in offering valuable services to high-income individuals without the fear that a disgruntled client's lawsuit will wipe out all the equity in the coach's home.

Limiting Liability through Insurance

Insurance is a second means by which coaches may limit their potential liability. With two means of limiting your liability, it is safer and wiser to use both options, rather than relying on one to the exclusion of the other. *Errors and omissions* insurance policies, which cover errors in connection with a professional practice, are the preferred method of protecting professionals such as lawyers, doctors, architects, and realtors. You may also wish to look into obtaining comprehensive general liability (CGL) insurance for your coaching practice as a means of limiting personal liability.

Self-Assessment Questionnaire

The type of business structure that makes most sense for your coaching practice emerges naturally from your answers to the following questions. Think in terms of how you see your practice growing during the next one to three years. Circle the answers that apply to your practice as a coach:

1. Do I operate a solo coaching practice, or have I combined forces with one or more other coaches?

   YES (I work solo.)

   NO (I've combined forces.)

2a. Does my coaching practice include any part- or full-time non-coach employees?

   YES (I have a non-coach part- or full-time office assistant or marketer.)

   NO (I answer my own phones, do my own typing, etc.)

2b. Can I get the occasional office assistance I need from a spouse or independent contractor instead of hiring an outsider?

   YES (I can get by with occasional help from my spouse or temporary agency.)

   NO (I really need, or will need, day-in, day-out help.)

3. If my coaching business incurs debts, such as a long-term lease, do I have personal assets that must be separated and protected from my business liabilities?

YES (Let's see, there's equity in my house, my auto is paid off, etc.)

NO (I'm flat broke, so I'm not worried about it.)

4. If I get sued in connection with my coaching practice, and my practice is exposed to catastrophic liability, do I have personal assets to safeguard from that liability?

    YES (Let's see, there's equity in my house, my auto is paid off, etc.)

    NO (I'm flat broke, so I'm not worried about it.)

5. Can I tolerate operating my practice out of my home, or do I really need an office outside the home?

    YES (I work from home.)

    NO (I have, or I really need, an office arrangement outside my home.)

6. Realistically, how much net income from coaching will I average for each of the next two years?

    1K to 30K (I'm just getting started or coaching part-time.)

    30K to 50K (I have an established coaching business, but I haven't hit the jackpot.)

    50K to 100K (I'm humming along quite well now.)

    100K+ (I'm really rockin' and rollin'.)

7. Does federal tax law provide me compelling reasons to set up my coaching practice as a corporation, so that I may take advantage of favorable tax treatment available only to corporations (favorable benefits include greater deductions for health-care premiums and out-of-pocket costs, etc.)?

YES (I have more than $100K in total income.)

NO (I have under $100K in total income.)

Sole Proprietorship

The sole proprietorship is the simplest and least costly business structure for low-risk enterprises. If you have no partners in your business (others who provide capital input, and who are entitled to a share of the profit), you're already a sole proprietorship by default until you take affirmative steps to register as a limited liability company or corporation. A sole proprietorship is probably right for you if you gave the following answers to the self-assessment questionnaire in the preceding section:

1-YES, 2a-NO, 2b-YES, 3-NO, 4-NO, 5-YES, 6–1K to 30K, and 7-NO

The primary downside of the sole proprietorship is that it exposes your personal assets to debts of the business and to potential lawsuits arising from business activities. If you have significant personal assets that could be exposed to business debt and lawsuits, you should operate your coaching practice as a limited liability company or corporation.

Partnership

If you share a percentage of your coaching profit with another coach or business partner, your state partnership law will probably label you as a partnership by default, even if you have operated on a handshake, and you have no formal, written partnership agreement. You can change from a partnership structure to a limited liability company or corporation by making the appropriate state filing with your Secretary of State. Alternatively, if you are simply sharing office space with another coach and not combining your separate coaching fees, you are operating as separate sole proprietorships.

Most states have adopted one or more variants of the Uniform Partnership Act. Partners can agree among themselves to be governed pretty much as they please. But if you do not reduce your partnership agreement to writing, your state's Partnership Act will govern your rights and responsibilities as partners, as well as your partnership's potential liability to others.

A partnership is probably the right structure if you gave the following answers to the self-assessment questionnaire in the preceding section:

1-NO, 2a-NO, 2b-YES, 3-NO, 4-NO, 5-YES, 6–1K to 30K, and 7-NO

The primary downside of the partnership business structure is that it exposes your personal assets to debts of the business (even if your partner incurred them without your explicit blessing), and to potential lawsuits arising from business activities (even those of your partner). If you have significant personal assets that could be exposed to business debt and lawsuits, you should operate your coaching practice as a limited liability company or corporation, and not as a partnership.

Corporation

Very rarely will a coaching practice need or want to operate as a corporation, unless there is a pressing need to insulate oneself and one's assets from liability. Operating as a corporation is a costly proposition. Corporations are designed so that capital can be raised from many sources, with each of those capital contributions being represented as shares of ownership.

Beyond the initial costs involved in setting up the corporation, you must consider the costs of ongoing compliance with various regulations that are designed to protect shareholders of large enterprises. When there is only one or, at most, a few shareholders, the corporate structure is overkill. Coaching practices do not require much in the way of start-up or operating capital, so there are generally no shareholders to protect, and no reason for going through the hassles of regulatory compliance.

Coaches may be tempted to form a so-called S corporation, one that pays its taxes through its individual owner or owners. However, regulatory burdens that apply to all corporations, large or small, are ordinarily too much for a small coaching practice to bear.

You should consider a corporation only if the answers to your self-assessment questionnaire are as follows:

1-NO, 2a-YES, 2b-NO, 3-YES, 4-YES, 5-NO, 6–100K+, and 7-YES

Limited Liability Company (LLC)

In recent years, the limited liability company (LLC) has become a popular hybrid structure for operating small businesses and professional practices. The LLC enables a coaching practice to adopt certain useful attributes of partnerships (without the personal liability), certain beneficial traits of corporations (without the regulatory red tape and double taxation), and certain unique attributes of its own that fit the needs of small businesses.

An LLC will probably meet your coaching practice needs if you answered the self-assessment questionnaire as follows:

1-YES or NO, 2a-YES or NO, 2b-YES or NO, 3-YES or NO, 4-YES or NO, 5-YES or NO, 6-Any Answer, 7-NO

Summary

Your coaching practice can be started on a shoestring as a sole proprietorship, so long as you're not overly concerned about exposing personal assets to business liabilities. As your coaching practice grows, you should seek legal advice and draft detailed understandings before you take on another coach as a partner or employee. Create an appropriate partnership agreement (if, with legal advice, you choose to operate as a partnership) or set of Articles of Organization (if, with legal advice, you choose to operate as an LLC). For a select series of articles dealing with business structures, check out http://www.entrepreneur.com/Your_Business/YB_Node/0,4507,143,00.html.

What Steps Should I Take to Select the Legal Name of My Coaching Practice?

> *"What's in a name? That which we call a rose/By any other name would smell as sweet."*
>
> —WILLIAM SHAKESPEARE, *ROMEO AND JULIET*

Shakespeare's Juliet showed little concern for names because, to Juliet, substance (true love) ought to prevail over form (family surnames, and the rivalries they represent). After all, a rose is still a rose, whatever it's called. But in twenty-first-century American commerce, a cavalier choice of name for your coaching practice can become a painful thorn; the rose might smell as sweet, but who wants a thorn in the side?

Overview of Legal Concerns in Naming Your Coaching Practice

Selecting a legal name for your coaching practice can be as simple or as complex as you choose to make it. The simplest name, from the legal standpoint, is the name your parents gave to you. I, personally, made the choice to name my coaching practice the Ash Grove Group, Inc. Admittedly, I might have saved considerable time, effort, and expense by simply naming my coaching practice William H. Lindberg, Professional Coach or Lindberg's Professional Coach Services. The name I chose was more fitting with the image I wished to create for my coaching practice.

Freedom to define the image and character of your professional practice is a significant part of the satisfaction you receive in operating a professional coaching practice. To exercise that freedom in a way that is fair to existing enterprises takes time, effort, and expense. To invent a distinctive name, and to verify that the chosen name does not infringe name-ownership rights of an established enterprise, can cost from hundreds to thousands of dollars. To many professional coaches, exercising the freedom to create a coaching practice name is worth it. Criteria to consider for name selection are those of availability, marketability, and durability.

Laws that affect business names have two primary objectives:

1. To provide disclosure to the public regarding the true identity of the business or service provider that the public is dealing with (in no small part, in case that business entity winds up in court).

189

2. To prevent freeloaders from taking unfair advantage of well-established business and trade names, particularly those names that have been fixed in the public's consciousness at great expense in promotional dollars. I could have named my coaching practice IBM Executive Coaching, but I would have risked sacrificing time spent with clients for time spent in court defending my use of those well-known letters, IBM. Most naming gaffes are not so blatant, but they can be just as costly.

The safest way to comply with laws that affect business and trade names is to use your family surname as the name of your coaching practice. But if you choose to use a name that you've invented for its unique marketing appeal or self-satisfying artistic license, please read on.

Sole Proprietors and Partnerships—Duty to Disclose "Fictitious Names" Used in Business

If the name of an enterprise does not match the name of the enterprise owner, the made-up enterprise name is known as a fictitious name, assumed name, or DBA (e.g., William H. Lindberg DBA "Ash Grove Group"). DBA stands for "doing business as." Owners of enterprises sporting fictitious, assumed, or DBA names must register the made-up name with either state or county officials, and they must publish notice of intent to use the made-up name locally. In most states, the names of corporations, LLCs, and limited partnerships must be filed with, and approved by, the state's Secretary of State at the time of incorporation or formation of the entity. Fictitious-name registration requirements apply primarily to sole proprietorships and partnerships since neither requires formal registration at the state level (you need a brief legal consultation with knowledgeable local counsel to be certain that this is the case in your state).

In most states, fictitious business names are registered and searched at the county, rather than state, level. For example, if you live in Los Angeles County, the search engine for locating fictitious names used in business within the county is found on the county's website at http://www.lavote.net/fbn/fbn.cfm. To find your county's website, go to www.naco.org, select About Counties, and then select Find a County. Also, check for the name you intend to use in your local phone book, both White and Yellow Pages.

Also look for fictitious-name search engines on the website of your home state's Secretary of State. For example, Florida has a statewide fictitious-name search engine at http://www.sunbiz.org /corpweb/inquiry/ficmenu.html. A link to your state's Secretary of State website is available at http://www.nass.org/busreg/corpreg .html. You may find it easier to run your fictitious name through a commercial search engine. Experian offers such a search engine at http://www.experian.com/business/fictitious_business_name.html. The cost of the Experian name search, at this writing, is a very reasonable $10. A generic form for filing a fictitious business name is available at http://www.ilrg.com/forms/vfictname.html. Or go to your county courthouse and ask for the office where fictitious business names should be filed.

The legal penalty for failing to properly register your fictitious name can be steep. For example, in Pennsylvania, failure to register a fictitious name can result in loss of your right to enforce a contract in the Pennsylvania courts, and at least $500 in additional fines. Further ramifications of failure to file a fictitious name are provided at http://www.e-magnify.com/articleview.asp?ID=541.

Equally important is the practical consequence of having to abandon a business name that was chosen too casually. Consider the cost of changing your listing in the Yellow Pages; reprinting your letterhead, business cards, office signs, brochures, and leaflets; and the cost, time, and embarrassment of notifying all your customers of your unfortunate initial choice of name. So what's in a name, Shakespeare? Plenty.

Trademarks, Trade Names, and Domain Names

A complex group of federal and state laws combine to protect business owners' exclusive rights to the use of their trademarks, trade names, and domain names. The names you choose to use in your practice cannot infringe others, just as others cannot infringe yours. Each form of so-called intellectual property provides, in essence, legal protection for the industriousness, marketing expense, and quality-control measures that you've built into your coaching practice. In accounting terms, trademarks, trade names, and domain names reflect and protect the goodwill of your professional practice. Trademarks, trade names, and domain names grant holders not just the right, but also the obligation, to prevent Johnny-come-latelies from using names or logos that customers might easily confuse with yours.

How much should you fret over infringing someone else's trademark or trade name? For most coaches, an expensive trademark search and legal opinion really are not necessary, unless you are tempting fate by using part of a well-known trademark (such as Kentucky Fried Coaching). Consider the consequences if you are forced to change your business name after making an ill-fated choice. If the name change would cost very little, and would have virtually no impact on your existing clients, you don't need to have a legal education in trademark, trade name, or domain name law. If you coach solo, it is highly improbable that a name change would have a serious impact on your practice. (For further guidance, see Elias, 2003.)

Do I Need a Business License to Practice as a Fee-Based Coach?

One or more types of licensing may apply to your coaching practice. In virtually all locations, you'll need a local business license; and in some states, you may also need to obtain a competency license at the state level. The purpose of competency licensing has less to do with taxes and more to do with protecting the unsuspecting public from charlatans and quacks in professional fields that require specialized knowledge, training, and skill, such as practicing law, medicine, or accounting, or with protecting the public from shoddy work by tradesmen, such as plumbers and electricians. Details concerning each form of licensing are provided in the next section.

Local Licensing Requirements That Apply to All Businesses

Counties and/or cities (especially larger cities) require businesses that operate within their boundaries to obtain a license to conduct business, and they do so primarily to collect a tax based on the projected or actual income of your coaching practice.

Compliance with local business licensing is a minor nuisance, but it also carries benefits. One benefit is to establish credibility with potential clients. Your local business license is one more plaque on your waiting room's wall, in case you're a coach who has fewer than three university degrees. Another practical benefit of the business license is to establish credit if you are self-employed (which some lenders define as deriving more than 50 percent of your income from a business of which you are a 25 percent or greater owner). Credit applications must often be accompanied by proof that you have practiced as a coach for two or more years. Business licenses and renewal certificates are often accepted as proof of two years' worth of self-employment.

To comply with local business-licensing requirements, first go to your local city hall (or town hall), and ask if you must obtain a license to conduct business at the city or town level. If not, city hall will direct you to the county office responsible for issuing business licenses.

Do I Need a State-Issued Professional License to Practice Coaching?

The International Coach Federation (ICF) Regulatory Committee has been carefully monitoring a possible trend for state legislators and regulators to define coaching as part of the regulated mental-health or professional-counseling fields. Approximately 40 states have statutory licensing boards for professional counselors. It is incumbent on coaches to personally examine state laws that define licensing requirements for those who are either mental-health professionals or professional counselors and consider whether their work falls within the ambit of such regulations. At the time of this writing, these developments are still unfolding, and it will be wise to keep abreast of future developments.

The ICF Regulatory Committee has also identified Washington and California as states in which it may be necessary to register with a state regulatory agency as unlicensed therapists or counselors. Also, New York passed a law in 2002 that defines mental-health practitioners broadly, making it possible that coaches will be treated as counselors, and thus require a state mental-health license, effective January 2005. If you live and practice in the states of Arizona, California, Florida, Minnesota, New York, or Washington, you should closely monitor legislation and rule making that affects mental-health practitioners. At the present time in Colorado, an explicit exemption has been granted placing these professionals outside of the mental-health regulatory framework: "The provisions of this article shall not apply to professional coaches who have had coach-specific training and who serve clients in the capacity of coaches" [CRS 12-43-215 (10)].

Do I Need a Formal Contract with Clients Who Retain Me?

"The faintest ink is more legible than the best memory."

—ANONYMOUS

In short, yes, you should enter into a written contract with each of your clients. At a very fundamental level, the process of reaching an agreement with a contract is to come to a meeting of the minds. When used in the context of professional services, this agreement is sometimes called an *engagement letter*. Professional coaches, like lawyers, architects, engineers, software programmers, and other professionals, need a somewhat detailed, written agreement for professional services. Once you have drafted this agreement and presented it to your client, it is wise to provide your client time to read the agreement, *amend it if necessary*, and sign it. Why have the client *amend* the agreement? If a dispute should arise with a client under the agreement, you will be able to show that you provided a fair opportunity for your client to read the contract and make changes. The amended agreement further shows that your client exercised the opportunity. The amendment your client suggests also shows equal bargaining power between you and your client. Courts tend to disfavor take-it-or-leave-it contracts, technically known as *contracts of adhesion*.

In addition to the formal, legal elements of a contract, such as

Coaching Agreement

This agreement, between _____ (client) and
_____ (coach) will begin on _____
and will continue for approximately _____ hour(s) per week/month for
a minimum of three months. The fee will be _____ per hour/month.

The coaching sessions are primarily conducted in person, in meetings that are typically from one to two hours in length each, and are supplemented by phone calls and emails. The coaching will concentrate on future options and choices of the client and will include training in the management of change, examination of core values, practicing life balance, exploring the assets of age and experience, identifying purpose and vision, and creating a plan for moving ahead. The coach promises to keep the information provided by the client confidential and private.

Upon completion of the three months, both the client and the coach will evaluate the relationship to see if the relationship should be extended or terminate. Even though the coach, William H. Lindberg, is an attorney, licensed to practice law in the State of Minnesota, this agreement does not include the rendering of legal services and no attorney-client relationship is formed hereby unless separately agreed in writing.

Conditions for success in a coaching relationship include accountability and a willingness to: Commit to completing homework between sessions. Commit to carrying out the action plan you create. Be on time for appointments. Commit to making the coaching relationship effective.

If the coaching relationship is not working as you desire, discuss this with me as your coach to make adjustments that will help in the achievement of optimal results.

View coaching as a value-added investment and commitment to make your goals and objectives happen.

Act with integrity in accordance with your stated values. Realize that the purpose of our interaction is to help you focus on and achieve your intentions and to support you in navigating the path you have chosen for yourself.

Our signatures on this agreement indicate an understanding of and agreement with the information outlined above.

_____   _____
Client   Coach
Date: _____   Date: _____

Figure 8.1 Sample of Coaching Agreement

Coach's Address

Sample Coaching Agreement—This is one sample of an agreement. It is not intended to be the only type of agreement.

To my client: Please review, adjust, sign where indicated, and return to me at the above address.

NAME _____

INITIAL TERM ____ MONTHS, FROM _____ THROUGH _____

FEE $_____ PER MONTH, $ _____ FOR THE PROJECT

SESSION DAY _____ SESSION TIME _____

NUMBER OF SESSIONS PER MONTH _____

DURATION _____ (length of scheduled session)

REFERRED BY: _____

GROUND RULES: 1. CLIENT CALLS THE COACH AT THE SCHEDULED TIME.
2. CLIENT PAYS COACHING FEES IN ADVANCE
3. CLIENT PAYS FOR LONG-DISTANCE CHARGES, IF ANY.

1. As a client, I understand and agree that I am fully responsible for my physical, mental and emotional well-being during my coaching calls, including my choices and decisions. I am aware that I can choose to discontinue coaching at any time.
2. I understand that "coaching" is a Professional-Client relationship I have with my coach that is designed to facilitate the creation/development of personal, professional or business goals and to develop and carry out a strategy/plan for achieving those goals.
3. I understand that coaching is a comprehensive process that may involve all areas of my life, including work, finances, health, relationships, education and recreation. I acknowledge that deciding how to handle these issues, incorporate coaching into those areas, and implement my choices is exclusively my responsibility.
4. I understand that coaching does not involve the diagnosis or treatment of mental disorders as defined by the American Psychiatric Association. I understand that coaching is not a substitute for counseling, psychotherapy, psychoanalysis, mental health care or substance abuse treatment and I will not use it in place of any form of diagnosis, treatment or therapy.
5. I promise that if I am currently in therapy or otherwise under the care of a mental health professional, that I have consulted with the mental health care provider regarding the advisability of working with a coach and that this person is aware of my decision to proceed with the coaching relationship.
6. I understand that information will be held as confidential unless I state otherwise, in writing, except as required by law.
7. I understand that certain topics may be anonymously and hypothetically shared with other coaching professionals for training OR consultation purposes.
8. I understand that coaching is not to be used as a substitute for professional advice by legal, medical, financial, business, spiritual or other qualified professionals. I will seek independent professional guidance for legal, medical, financial, business, spiritual or other matters. I understand that all decisions in these areas are exclusively mine and I acknowledge that my decisions and my actions regarding them are my sole responsibility.

I have read and agree to the above.

_____ Client Signature   Date:_____

Figure 8.1 *Continued*

offer, acceptance, and *consideration* (a formal legal term relating to exchange of mutual value in the contracting process), there are a number of considerations to address about how the coaching process will work. Some coaches refer to this process as designing the alliance with the client, and this phrase aptly communicates the goal of the contracting process. Even though his description of contracting comes from a consulting perspective, Block (2000) offers an eloquent description of the formal and informal contracting process.

Written agreements for coaching services, in and of themselves, dramatically reduce the chance of a dispute when your client receives the bill. Therefore, you increase the likelihood you will be paid. If your dispute should end up in small claims or an even higher court, your written agreement will give you legal legs to stand on.

Figure 8.1 provides two samples of professional coaching agreements, based on the contract I have used for several years in my practice and a coaching agreement from the International Coach Federation website. These agreements are merely illustrative, and an agreement suitable for your type of coaching practice is important to craft in the context of the type of work you do.

Another best practice among coaches is to incorporate a code of ethics addendum to your coaching agreement and discuss the reasons you have chosen to include these ethical guidelines in your work. Provisions in such a code of ethics frequently include discussions of confidentiality, qualifications, referral options, boundary issues, and so on. The ICF code of ethics offers guidance in many of these basic ethical principles in the coaching arena.

At What Point Should I Hire an Attorney for My Coaching Practice?

In spite of all the lawyer jokes you may have heard, sooner or later every businessperson needs competent legal advice, and so do you in connection with your coaching practice. Even people trained as lawyers sometimes need a lawyer, lest they suffer the fate wherein lawyers who represent themselves have a fool for a client, as the common saying goes. One of the most important functions of seeking legal advice is to obtain competent, objective, disinterested counsel.

Among the most important services a lawyer can provide is preventative law. By consulting with a lawyer early in your business development, you may be able to avoid much more serious problems later. Consider the expenditure of funds to receive capable legal advice early as a combination of a good investment and an insurance policy. A lawyer should be viewed as a key member of your board of advisors. Along with your accountant and marketing advisor, your lawyer is a critical part of your resource team. Essentially, you, as the client, are the quarterback of this team, but you can function in a much more informed and knowledgeable way when you know your legal options and can make a conscious choice about those options.

When Do I Really Need a Lawyer?

In a society and business environment as complex as ours is today, functioning as a business many times requires sound legal advice. Among the common business situations in which legal counsel is well advised for coaching practices are the following:

- ◆ When finalizing the business structure for your coaching practice

- ◆ Before you finalize the form contract you will use for client assignments

- ◆ Before you sign a major contract or a lease (for office space, large assignments, etc.)

- When you hire employees or anyone you expect to pay more than $600 (to review employment agreement, to understand your tax and other reporting obligations as an employer)
- Before you undertake a joint venture or partnership
- When you need to protect intellectual property you have developed in the course of your practice (trademarks and copyrights)

How Do I Find a Good Lawyer?

Finding a trusted advisor to help you navigate legal terrain can be a daunting task; it is also a highly personal decision. Although different people will approach this task using different methods, the following guidelines will help to demystify the process and make it less intimidating.

Step 1: Gathering Candidate Names

Referrals from friends or colleagues are often a sound method of developing a list of potential lawyers to handle your routine business matters. Lawyers, like doctors, have become highly specialized, so you will need to match your immediate need with the correct field of legal specialization. For general advice relating to your coaching practice, retain a lawyer with at least five years of experience who has many small businesses as clients.

By calling the attorney referral service of your state or county bar association, you can obtain names of attorneys who serve as small-business counselors. You can also consult Yellow Pages advertising; but remember, you are still at the name-gathering stage. Finally, you can gather names of candidate attorneys from the following online sources:

West's Legal Directory (www.findlaw.com)

Martindale-Hubbell (www.martindale-hubbell.com)

Public libraries also carry a printed directory of lawyers called the *Martindale-Hubbell Law Directory*. This publication, like its online counterpart, offers peer ratings of attorneys, information about their educational backgrounds, articles they have written, and representative clients. Look for attorneys who have AV ratings. The AV rating reflects the opinion of fellow attorneys that the listed attorney is competent and ethical.

Some states have specialization certification, wherein lawyers have demonstrated to a certification board that they have deeper knowledge and experience in a particular specialized area of law. Depending on your legal needs, such as trademark advice, for example, certification as a specialist can help you decide on a lawyer.

Step 2: Interviewing Your Candidate Lawyers

Meeting with your prospective lawyer candidates can be an intimidating experience. Remember, in the attorney–client relationship, you, the client, are the boss. You are seeking the advice of a lawyer and expertise in legal matters, but you are the decision maker. You should set aside time to interview no fewer than two candidates, but three is better.

Here is a checklist of questions you should ask during your interviews:

- Does the lawyer have at least five years' experience representing clients with needs like yours?

- Can the lawyer refer you to several clients with legal needs similar to yours who can vouch they were satisfied with services provided?

- What fee arrangements does the lawyer propose?

- Does the lawyer have a written engagement agreement that describes how services are provided and what fees and incidental costs will be charged?

- Is the lawyer amenable to working with your other advisors, such as your CPA?

- Can the lawyer give you an estimate of the total cost of your project or legal matter?

Step 3: Making Your Choice

After meeting your prospective lawyer, reflect on how the meeting went:

- Do you feel comfortable with this lawyer as an individual?

- Are you comfortable with the lawyer's experience in the area in which you need counsel?

- Does the lawyer give you the opportunity to ask probing questions?

- Can you afford this lawyer or law firm?

Remember, you are not bound for life to continue working with the attorney you initially select. But the more time, effort, and care you spend making an initial selection of legal counsel, the easier it will be to focus on your coaching practice, and you will sleep better knowing that you have another ally in business with you.

Why Should I Worry about Intellectual Property?

Coaches deal not only in the domain of emotional issues, but also in the domain of behavior and cognitive issues. In the course of coaching an individual, a team, or a group, a coach frequently will develop, and certainly use, copyrighted material.

Included in the ICF code of ethics are the following provisions:

Professional Conduct at Large

3. I will respect different approaches to coaching. I will honor the efforts and contributions of others and not misrepresent them as my own.

In addition to these provisions in the code of ethics, there are quite specific and detailed legal requirements regarding the protection of intellectual property, including copyrighted works, trademarks, and the like. A detailed discussion of these matters is beyond the scope of this chapter, but several excellent resources are noted in the Additional Resources list at the end of the chapter.

What Type(s) of Insurance Should I Have?

Coaches typically need property, liability, disability, auto, and other forms of insurance. (See Kelley, 2003 for a more complete coverage of this topic.) Professional liability insurance deserves special mention, not only because the stakes are high, but also because this aspect of insurance can easily be misunderstood. Why bother? The rationale may be as simple as that doing so will allow you to sleep better at night, knowing your assets are protected and that you have anticipated the cost of your legal defense if a lawsuit should arise. At this point, the insurance landscape for coaches is quite unsettled. Because coaching as a distinct field is so new, the lack of experience (such as claims history) with the pool of insureds makes underwriting these policies difficult.

Best Practices

This section highlights some best practices to attend to in your coaching practice. These areas are by no means exhaustive of the facets of your work that require attention. Rather, they are illustrative of the aspects of a coach's practice that can support and lend structure to effective coaching. In many ways, adhering to these practices will help to keep you centered, grounded, and fully present as you deliver coaching to clients.

The code of ethics of the International Coach Federation serves as a set of specific guidelines that articulate the ICF's philosophy of coaching, definition of coaching, the standards of ethical conduct, and a pledge of ethics. A detailed analysis of each of these provisions is beyond the scope of this chapter. Moreover, these guidelines are continuing to evolve, so a professional coach is well advised to keep apprised of changes to these guidelines and additional material, which will further interpret and clarify the standards of conduct for coaches. The ICF's code of ethics is found in Appendix A in this book and at the website of the International Coach Federation at www.coachfederation.org/eweb.

Record Keeping

At the slightest hint that something may be going awry in a coach–client relationship, it becomes even more imperative that you keep good records and document your activity in the coaching relationship. The discipline of maintaining good records is vital and may help if you ever become a defendant or need to testify in court.

Presumably, if you have attended an accredited coach-training program, one aspect of your training will include documenting a client relationship over time (in essence, a longitudinal case study). By incorporating this discipline into your practice, you are prepared if you ever need to defend a particular action you took in a coaching relationship. Admittedly, needing to document your actions seems contradictory to holding a client in a place of unconditional positive regard; yet from a professional practice perspective, it is indeed a prudent approach. Moreover, documentation can be part of holding your client accountable for his expressed goals.

Confidentiality

Chapter 5, "Developing and Maintaining Client Trust," offers a much more thorough treatment of the issue of confidentiality, but this issue is worth mentioning in a more general treatment of legal issues and coaching. A nearly universal tenet is that conversations and subject matter of a coach–client relationship are understood to be confidential. Despite this nearly universal understanding, what are the limits of confidentiality? The ICF code of ethics states:

22. I will respect the confidentiality of my client's information, except as otherwise authorized by my client, or as required by law.

23. I will obtain agreement with my clients before releasing their names as clients or references or any other client identifying information.

24. I will obtain agreement with the person being coached before releasing information to another person compensating me.

Protecting Confidentiality by Asserting Privilege

At the time of this writing, no recognized coach–client privilege is comparable to attorney–client privilege, priest–penitent privilege, doctor–patient privilege, and so on. Thus, if a coach were somehow required to testify in a lawsuit through the subpoena process, the coach would be required to testify or face the possible risk of contempt of court, unless a judge could be persuaded that a coach–client privilege existed.

Emerging Issues

As codes of ethics emerge, as more and more coaches seek formal coach training, and as practices develop, the field of coaching appears to be gaining increasing momentum as a discrete profession. Among the traditional attributes of a profession are elements such as a well-defined body of knowledge and expertise, and widely accepted and adopted ethical principles. As codes of conduct develop in a profession, one by-product that emerges is something in tort law known as a standard of care. If one gains a particular credential in the field of coaching and represents oneself as a master certified coach, there is a strong likelihood that the bar, in effect, will be higher and that the holder of such a credential will need to coach in a manner consistent with the requisite standard of care and competency of a coach holding such a credential. One way to maintain competence and uphold the standard of care is by continued education.

Professional Continuing Education Issues

Another aspect of credibility for a new field such as coaching is how coaching intersects with other, more established fields. The following case arose in a somewhat arcane area regarding continuing education credit for lawyers: *Ash Grove Group v. Minnesota Board of*

Continuing Legal Education (Minnesota Supreme Court docket number C2-84-2163), 2003.

The subject of the seminar was career satisfaction for judges and lawyers. After several years of wrangling over credits at the administrative level (the Board of Continuing Legal Education), the sponsor of the program eventually sued the CLE Board, and the matter was argued in the Minnesota Supreme Court in September 2003. The key issue was whether a coaching-style seminar that involved seminar attendees in coaching exercises grounded in adult development was "directly related to the practice of law" or simply personal development and thus not eligible for CLE credit. Ultimately, the Minnesota Supreme Court essentially acknowledged the validity of the coaching component of the seminar and issued a more expansive rule that accommodated courses such as the one in question. (See Keeva, 2004.)

Marketing and Hype

Coaches can get in both ethical and legal hot water by overstating credentials or capabilities. The ICF code of ethics states: "I will accurately identify my level of coaching competence, and I will not overstate my qualifications, expertise, or experience as a coach."

The law allows a certain amount of puffing in the sale of goods or services, but excessive braggadocio about the benefits of coaching can be elevated in court to a warranty of results, or even charges of deceptive trade practices if outlandish benefits or outcomes from coaching are promised.

The Uniform Commercial Code attributes an implied warranty to the sale of goods. By analogy, if your website or direct-mail piece, in effect, assures a superb outcome with every coaching relationship, a court could imply that superb results were either expressly or impliedly warranted. Coaching outcomes, of course, are highly variable, so do not oversell outcomes in your promotional materials.

Focus instead on *processes* that provide *opportunities* for personal growth and development, and the guiding hand that the coach provides in helping clients realize those opportunities.

Application

In the following scenario, we present a case that highlights several issues that frequently occur in executive coaching sessions. Among the issues that arise in this scenario are the demands of a client's role in an organization, the political context in which a coaching relationship happens, competing demands of personal and work commitments, the sometimes fuzzy boundaries between coaching and therapy, and the ever-present array of ethical issues that may surface during and after coaching engagements.

Case Study

You have been retained to coach the senior vice president of marketing for a Fortune 500 company, MEGA Telecom, hereinafter Mega. This organization has a fairly well-established coaching culture and has retained you to enhance the performance of Senior VP, or SVP, an individual who has risen meteorically through the organization, and who had previously demonstrated incredible success at other companies. There has been a cost, however. SVP has become legendary for her authoritarian management style. The CEO has observed that the approach of SVP has been causing havoc on the leadership team because of her blind spots and lack of empathy for other members of the organization. Moreover, during the most recent coaching session, the client shares with you that her marriage is foundering, and she has had very little time with her two children. In essence, the nanny knows her children much better than she.

The CEO is willing to retain you but wants regular status reports regarding how the coaching is going and your periodic assessment of how the client is responding to the coaching.

Your client is perennially preoccupied with the political structure of the organization and attempts to pump you for any valuable inside information you might have about the CEO's disposition between marketing and R&D—the two divisions have had a tumultuous relationship over the past several years.

The organization has retained you to develop a better team sense and cooperative atmosphere among members of the leadership team. The corporation is your client, and you are working with SVP. The corporation has an employee assistance program for all employees.

You sense the client may have some issues with depression and stress related to meeting this quarter's goals. The organization also has a code of conduct for all employees that specifies appropriate business practices. Your client has indicated a certain sense of impunity toward some of these standards and, in your view, appears to be ready to take some shortcuts that, in your opinion, while not illegal, would be a clear violation of the company's code of conduct. Among the items you have contracted with the client for are improved productivity and team cohesion at the company.

Questions

1. What obligations of confidentiality are owed, and to whom?
2. Should you as the coach consider a referral for your client to a therapist?
3. In the past, you have also coached at another telecommunications company that has announced a product line in direct competition with your current client. You

(Continued)

are not currently coaching anyone at the competitor company. Does this situation pose a conflict of interest such that you should withdraw?

4. If you have been retained by the organization to do performance coaching, how much latitude do you have to delve into the client's relationship with her spouse and family?

5. For purposes of this example, you are not trained or certified as a marriage or family therapist. Is delving into this area merely functioning effectively as a holistic coach, or does this create a boundary issue outside the scope of your contract with MEGA Telecom?

REFERENCES

Block, P. (2000). *Flawless consulting: A guide to getting your expertise used* (2nd ed.). San Francisco: Jossey Bass.

Elias, S. (2003). *Trademark: Legal care for your business and product name.* Berkeley, CA: Nolo Press.

Hudson, F.M. (1999). *The handbook of coaching: A comprehensive guide for managers, executives, consultants, and human resource professionals.* San Francisco: Jossey Bass.

Keeva, S. (2004). CLE for the whole person. *American Bar Association Journal, 76.*

Kelley, D. (2003). *The business of coaching: A comprehensive guide to starting and growing your coaching practice.* Salinas, CA: Clarity in Action.

Shapiro, F. (1993). *The Oxford dictionary of American legal quotations* (p. ix). New York: Oxford University Press.

Williams, P., & Davis, D.C. (2002). *Therapist as life coach: Transforming your practice.* New York: W.W. Norton.

ADDITIONAL RESOURCES

The resources listed here are merely a sampling of a wide array available. Rather than overwhelm the reader, the purpose of this annotated list is to provide a starting point for high-quality tools in the area of law and coaching. Most of these tools, in turn, include rich bibliographic resources. Inasmuch as Internet search engines, such as Google and Yahoo, are becoming increasingly sophisticated, using the technology available for your research can help with specific inquiries. Moreover, governmental websites are offering an ever-increasing amount of primary legal materials online, as well as providing tools to help streamline your search.

Besenjak, C. (2001). *Copyright plain & simple* (2ⁿᵈ ed.). Franklin Lakes, NJ: Career Press.

> Very readable explanation of basic intellectual-property concepts, with an emphasis on copyright law.

Bloomsbury Publishing PLC (2004). *The ultimate small business guide: A resource for startups and growing businesses.* Cambridge, MA: Basic Books.

> Comprehensive compendium of action lists, directories, resources, checklists, and planning tools that affect small businesses.

Boulay, D.-N., & Pohlman, K.J. (2003). *The entrepreneur's legal guide: Strategies for starting, marketing and making your small business profitable.* Naperville, IL: Sphinx Publishing.

> Offers tips, legal alerts, questions, and resources to allow readers to consider the unique aspects of their own situations. Avoids the cookie-cutter approach that sometimes afflicts this type of publication.

Carter, G.W. (2003). *J.K. Lasser's taxes made easy for your home-based business* (5ᵗʰ ed.). Hoboken, NJ: John Wiley & Sons.

A practical handbook for self-employed individuals, whether sole proprietors, partnerships, or corporate entities. Offers a realistic, thorough discussion of the choice of business form, as well as references to the Internal Revenue Code, regulations, and key legal decisions.

DuBoff, L.D. (2004). *The law (in plain English) for small business.* Naperville, IL: Sphinx Publishing.

Exceptionally clear and accurate descriptions of commonly encountered legal questions that affect small businesses. This text contains expanded coverage of several topics found in this chapter, such as contract and intellectual-property issues.

Elias, S., & Stim, R. (2001). *Patent, copyright & trademark: An intellectual property desk reference* (4th ed.). Berkeley, CA: Nolo Press.

Comprehensive collection of definitions, statutes, forms, and text to help readers navigate the complex world of intellectual property.

Floyd, P.M. (2003). Counseling the unlicensed counselor. *Hennepin Lawyer 72,* 22–25.

Excellent and insightful analysis of the Unlicensed Counselor Law recently enacted in Minnesota. Although its emphasis is on the Minnesota Statute, the commentary applies to the settings in other states where legislation has been pending or enacted.

Garner, B.A. (Ed.). (1999). *Black's law dictionary* (7th ed.). St. Paul, MN: West.

This classic resource is perhaps the most widely sold single volume about law in the United States. The dictionary provides a basic foundation for deciphering the vocabulary of the law, which is a fundamental requirement of understanding legal concepts.

Irving, S., & Michon, K. (2000). *Nolo's encyclopedia of everyday law: Answers to your most frequently asked legal questions.* Berkeley, CA: Nolo.

Broad-based coverage of a wide variety of personal and business-related legal issues. This text provides basic, straightforward answers to frequently asked questions about legal issues.

Sharma, P. (1999). *The Harvard Entrepreneur's Club guide to starting your own business.* New York: John Wiley & Sons.

A manual designed to fuel and support entrepreneurial energy. This text provides not only an overview of the context for setting up a business, but also a perspective of the legal, economic, and regulatory climate that affects entrepreneurs.

Shea, B., & Haupt, J. (1995). *Entrepreneur Magazine small business legal guide.* New York: John Wiley & Sons.

Somewhat dated, but still useful as a sourcebook for forming and managing a small business.

Steingold, F.S. (2003). *Legal guide for starting and running a small business* (7th ed.). Berkeley, CA: Nolo.

One of the best and most current resources available at a modest price for a fairly comprehensive guide.

Warda, M. (1998). *How to register your own copyright* (2nd ed.). Naperville, IL: Sphinx Publishing.

Resource guide covering the legal issues and procedures to register your copyrighted material, complete with appropriate forms from the U.S. Copyright Office.

Whitworth, L., Kimsey-House, H., & Sandahl, P. (1998). *Co-active coaching: New skills for coaching people toward success in work and life.* Palo Alto, CA: Davies-Black.

Excellent overall coaching resource with numerous forms, coaching agreements, and tools to assist in the management of a coaching practice.

Williams, P., & Davis, D.C. (2002). *Therapist as life coach: Transforming your practice*. New York: W.W. Norton.

A resource to better understand the demarcation between coaching and therapy. The description of the history and evolution of life coaching is especially useful to understanding the background and distinctions between the fields of psychotherapy, counseling, and coaching.

9

The Intersection of
Culture and Ethics

Marilyn O'Hearne and Charles Hamrick

Objective

This chapter discusses how culture affects ethical and moral standards; this phenomenon, then, requires coaches to expand their personal approaches to coaching people of different cultures. We examine the interaction of cultural differences and ethics in coaching, and the effects of this interaction on coaching cross-culturally. We propose that no one ethic pervades all cultures, and that it is the coach's responsibility to discern nonjudgmentally those situations, attitudes, and behaviors that reflect ethical dilemmas. We discuss frameworks for understanding cultural values, and how those values drive ethics, and we make distinctions between cultural and individual values in coaching. A key consideration is who will do how much adjusting (client/coach, host/visiting culture, etc.) when it comes to intercultural variances, including ethics.

Pre-Chapter Self-Assessment Test

Answer on a scale of one (1) to five (5), with one (1) being *strongly disagree* and five (5) being *strongly agree*:

1. I understand the customs and values of my own culture.

2. I understand the customs and values of at least one other culture, different from my own.

3. I feel comfortable with people of different backgrounds.

4. I enjoy learning about other cultures.

5. I demonstrate patience and understanding with people who do not speak my native language.

6. I apologize when I do or say something that offends someone of a different culture.

7. I do not respond to slurs or jokes directed at others' expense.

8. I seek the company of others who are different from me.

9. I enjoy working in a multicultural environment or team.

10. When interacting with others from a different culture, I seek to understand their reactions to my behavior, and to make adjustments accordingly.

11. I enjoy building relationships with people from other cultures.

12. I am alert to stereotypes of other cultures.

13. I assume responsibility when others do not understand what I am saying.

14. I resist blaming others when something goes wrong.

Introduction

Culture is the galaxy of unique shared beliefs, values, communication styles, and behaviors that differentiate one group from another. Sources of a group's culture include the land upon which the group members live, their history, their family models, and their socioeconomic and political environments. As humans, we learn from these environments to behave in certain ways, and we often judge the world by what is familiar.

The effects of culture are that we all experience discrimination and stereotypes, but money and power can buffer us from the effects of discrimination. The outcomes of culture are that we tend to seek the company of those most familiar to ourselves, and we resist change and the unfamiliar. As Edward W. Said remarked in *Culture and Resistance*, "Culture is a way of fighting against extinction and obliteration" (2002).

When coaching someone from a different culture, coaches may unknowingly engage in inappropriate behavior unless they are culturally aware. To be culturally aware means not only to become familiar with clients personally and professionally, but also with their culture. It also means coaches must be aware of their own culture, the potential differences between their culture and that of their clients, and how those differences might have an ethical impact upon the coaching relationship.

Even within one country, cultural diversity exists. Cultural groupings occur through geography (nation, region), profession, gender, religion, social system (social class, family, organization, ethnicity), and physical ability. Businesses, governments, and societies are sometimes governed by diverse and ambiguous rules of conduct. As coaches, we interrelate with people who face dilemmas daily as a result of these ambiguities, and we have a responsibility to create an environment in which these individuals can access behaviors and attitudes that will work and are appropriate for the culture. For example, persuasion in the United States is often considered strength, but in Japan is considered rude. There are also differences in corporate culture as to the amount of persuasion that is acceptable. As coaches we meet people who have to manage in such environments and may not understand how to do so. We must create an environment in which they can understand that there are differences, and that to be effective they need to adapt.

Ethics and morals are often cited as what determine the appropriateness of an action; however, ethics and morals mean different things for different people. For *ethics*, philosophers explore concepts, dilemmas, and theories of good; while most of us, knowingly or otherwise, establish or define operational *standards* for proper, fair behavior when dealing with others.

Morals are often described as a set of rules that govern behaviors considered to be good by the majority of rational members of a given society. The rub is that moral standards covering all behaviors vary depending upon the society or situation. Bribery is often cited as an example of the culturally dependent nature of moral standards because bribery is considered illegal in many cultures, but is viewed in others as a legitimate commission for participating in a business transaction. As discussed later, this view of bribery as legitimate has ethical limitations.

A more mundane, but relevant, example of the variability among moral standards involves stopping at a red light late at night. In China, for example, one most likely would go through the light, based on a value system that rewards pragmatism—whatever works. In the United States, one might stop or go, depending upon the individual's personal sense of balance between risk-taking and what is considered fair. No harm, no foul. In Japan, one might wait for the light to change, with the decision not dependent upon fear of breaking a rule, but rather upon consideration about being shamed, even by someone unknown to the individual. In Germany, one is likely to obey the red light signal and stop, simply because to do so is a rule.

Ethics may take multiple forms. Consider ethics based upon principles. Principles are supposedly indisputable and not to be compromised. No individual personal judgments about good-bad-right-wrong are considered valid. Common examples of principles might be to not lie or steal; or following the maxim, "The ends do not justify the means." On lying and stealing, Mark Twain once said, "If opportunity and desire came at the same time, who would escape the gallows?" Telling white lies or taking a few paper clips home from work does not necessarily make us unethical persons, and a white lie may be for a greater good. On the question of the ends justifying the means, there are tremendous variations in the weight ascribed by various cultures to this principle. To the Chinese, pragmatism is a core value—it does not matter whether the cat is black or white, as long as it catches mice. To an American, it is how you play the game, although recent corporate malfeasance and sports drug scandals seem to undermine this maxim. Unfortunately, applying the concept of principled ethics often avoids dilemmas instead of resolving them. We explore this issue interculturally later in the chapter.

Another form of ethics goes beyond relying on principles. Based upon respect for humanity, this type recognizes that dilemmas exist in the real world. This form, sometimes termed *applied ethics*, relies on appropriate individual judgment, encourages personal responsibility, seeks awareness of applicable moral standards, and stresses compliance with these components. This form allows for deviation from principled ethics when such deviation is for the legitimate benefit of others—for the benefit of humankind.

Applied ethics is not to be confused with *situational ethics*: "This is the way we do it here." In situational ethics, each person decides what seems to be the right thing to do, without reference to the moral standards of the majority. Situational ethics allows almost anything.

Ethical behavior is not always expressly mandated in workplaces, given the evidence, although the authors have reviewed many corporate ethical guidelines translated into multiple languages. Implicit guidelines, however, are unsatisfactory, particularly with respect to collective and corporate actions. Often, the responsibility for ethical behavior is somehow assumed to belong to the boss; however, this responsibility must be resident at all levels in the organization for effectiveness.

The Interaction between Culture and Ethics: The Cultural Iceberg

If you have studied Freud's psychoanalytic theory, you remember the iceberg effect as applied to the conscious/unconscious mind. What we are conscious of is just the tip of the iceberg. And so in cultures: what we can observe through our senses—behaviors, language, dress, art, customs—is the tip of the iceberg (see Figure 9.1).

Below the surface are the cultural values that drive the behaviors. *Values* are what people hold to be important. In some cultures, a value might be achievement; in others, relationships. The values a culture holds will affect what behaviors are appropriate (ethical) and acted upon.

The base of the iceberg represents a culture's shared beliefs. A culture that believes in fate or luck will have different values and behaviors from a culture that believes people determine the direction of their lives through their choices.

As coaches, we join with our clients in identifying their personal values, which say something about who they are as an individual. Cultural values relate to who we are as members of a cultural group; a norm or standard of what is considered ethically right. *Individual values* represent what individuals desire; *cultural values*, what the group desires.

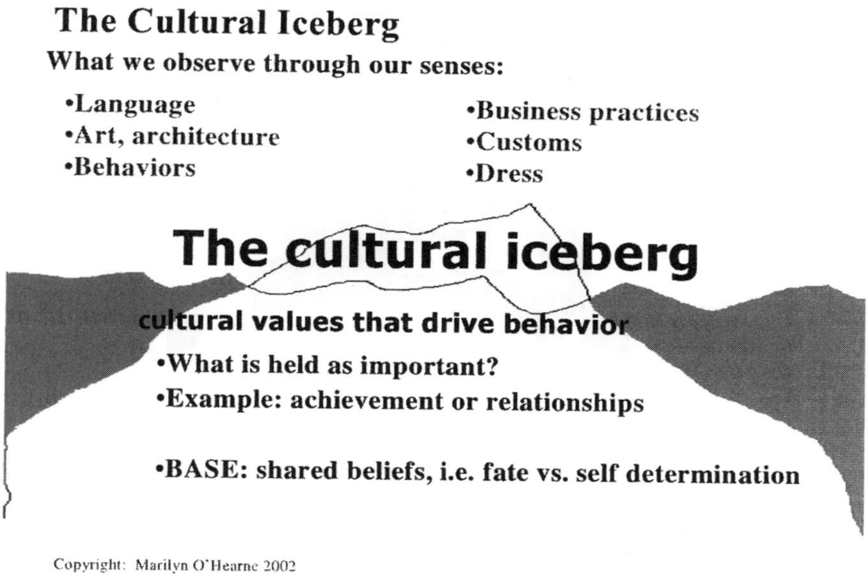

The Cultural Iceberg

What we observe through our senses:

- Language
- Art, architecture
- Behaviors

- Business practices
- Customs
- Dress

The cultural iceberg

cultural values that drive behavior

- What is held as important?
- Example: achievement or relationships

- BASE: shared beliefs, i.e. fate vs. self determination

Copyright: Marilyn O'Hearne 2002

Figure 9.1 The Cultural Iceberg

To be effective coaching interculturally, we need to understand and, especially with teams, to integrate and leverage cultural differences. But where do we draw the ethical line? Who does the adjusting, how much, and when? For example, while teaching an Organizational Behavior and International Business course in Hong Kong and Malaysia, students' answers to discussion questions on preferred management practices were different from the U.S. textbook's answers because the students' culture is more collective than individualistic. The Hong Kong/Malaysia culture emphasizes "we"—what is good for the group—rather than "I"—what is good for me. What may be seen as good and ethical business practices in one culture may not be considered so in another. It is the coach's responsibility to take the initiative to understand, note, and articulate differences.

The Relevance of Coaching to Culture and Ethics

Basic principles of coaching lend themselves well to intercultural environments. First, the highly personalized process of coaching supports the infinite range of possible situations in which persons might find themselves. Next, the process is specifically designed to bring about learning, effective action, and performance improvement, which then leads to personal growth for the individual, as well as better business results for the organization.

Coaching is specifically designed to build the person's level of awareness and personal responsibility for actions and behaviors, while providing structure and feedback in a collaborative process between the coach and key players within the organization. This involvement, while maintaining confidentiality, unleashes the individual's potential to meet personal and organizational goals and objectives.

Organizations tend to choose employees who learn best from new experiences and place them in multicultural settings. These new environments might include international work, overseas assignments, and multicountry alliances. In the throes of being in a new environment, employees are also possibly dealing with negotiations, culture shock, and how to manage diversity. Research seems to suggest that learning in a different culture occurs best when certain strategies are in place for the learner. These strategies include listening well, communicating openly and clearly, solving problems, and accepting responsibility for one's own behavior while exploring new environments.

As a coach adjusts to a new culture (because of the assignment) or helps a client adjust to a new culture, it is helpful to remember that learning moves in two directions:

1. Lessons learned can be of a personal, business, and relational nature. *Personal lessons* might include knowing and managing personal behavior while balancing family and work. *Business*

lessons might include running international businesses and linking personal development to the business initiatives and cultural environment. *Relational lessons* might include adapting to multicultural environments and leading people unlike oneself.

2. Learning occurs in competencies, especially those related to working in intercultural environments. Such competencies include establishing credibility, valuing others, demonstrating adaptability and flexibility, networking, negotiating, and a having a global mind-set.

Coaches can remind themselves and help their clients to recognize that intercultural competencies motivate people to break out of their own cultural mind-sets and begin exploring new cultures and those cultures' social customs and systems. For example, having intercultural communication competencies also enables people to work together to solve common problems and achieve organizational objectives.

As a point of clarification, integrating into another culture is *not* abandoning one's own ideas and values in exchange for wholly absorbing or accepting those of another culture (just as it is not prudent to leave your own toothbrush and comb at home on a trip, and expect to use those of the host where you stay). Rather, integrating into another culture means critiquing one's own cultural values and norms, learning and critiquing the norms and values of another culture, transcending one's own culture, and then internalizing appropriately those valued perspectives one has gained from a different culture. This process goes beyond integration and actually provides for the possibility of personal transformation.

Bringing Ethics into the Coaching Environment

As mentioned previously, *ethics* is a method of determining right and wrong, and *morality* is a system of practices that produce conformity of behavior within a community. Many cultures believe the individual is primary, and so ethics supersede morality. Other, more communitarian, cultures believe a system of morality is critical to cultural survival.

In addition, theories of morality or ethics state that we have the duty to bring about the greatest good overall, and that we are required not to deceive others with whom we have social partnerships. An example of operating from the belief that one has a moral and ethical duty to bring about the greatest good overall would be a situation in which a person comes in to his manager and states that his wife has a serious illness, but the HR policies do not cover the expense of medicines that would cure her. The question to the coach would be how to motivate the client to explore possibilities that would solve the dilemma of deciding between aiding one person and adhering to policies that reflect the common good. An example that represents the moral/ethical requirement not to deceive others is that of corporate governance and transparency, which we explore next.

Governance

Governance, transparency, and *leadership* are each spokes of the rudder that steers organizations through legal, ethical, and moral opportunists who seem to be waiting at every corner. *Governance* is the process by which an organization or society conducts its behavior, both internal and public. Transparency is about involvement. It means to communicate in such a way that stakeholders in what you are doing (corporate or otherwise) are involved. Leadership has many definitions: the one we are referring to is the ability of people to create an environment in which they can create their own (and the company's) destiny. Develop one of the three, and you will likely achieve the other two. Governance is internal, in that it defines the manner in which power and creativity are used within the organization. It is to this end that coaching most benefits the organization: shaping the individual's response to the ever-changing environment.

Governance has many faces throughout the globe. For example, in the United States, governance is upheld through complex balances between government regulation and shareholder power. In Japan, though, the complex systems of relationship and obligation, consensus building, and peer review provide a form of governance that from the outside might seem cumbersome and sluggish. Some Japanese companies have changed to more effective governance systems; but cultural internal processes remain largely intact. Chinese companies depend heavily on relationships to provide governance; however, beauty is in the eye of the beholder, and in this culture shared ownership, the board, and management often work against the levels of transparency needed to provide confidence to the outside investor.

As leadership and governance models become more horizontal, power is shared with others throughout the organization, which requires higher levels of cooperation and transparency. In periods of change, and in intercultural settings as companies decentralize, people are often reluctant to give up power. In many cultures, coaching can play a strategic role in the development of leaders that foster the required transparency and cooperation in decentralized multicultural organizations. The coach can support leadership transformation by working with individuals to expand competencies of empathy, openness, tolerance, and flexibility.

The Legal Environment

The U.S Congress enacted the Foreign Corrupt Practices Act (FCPA) in 1977 after Securities and Exchange Commission investigations during the mid-1970s revealed that more than 400 companies had paid questionable or illegal payments in excess of $300 million to foreign government officials and politicians. Under the law, executives can go to jail, and companies can be fined and barred from government procurement contracts, for infractions of the law.

To avoid legal consequences, many firms have implemented detailed compliance programs intended to detect and prevent any improper payments by employees and agents, and to reflect accurately the transactions of the corporation through internal accounting controls. Most large global companies stipulate zero-tolerance toward infractions relating to the FCPA.

Although Congress originally enacted the FCPA to restore public confidence in the integrity of the American business system, Congress became concerned that American companies were operating at a disadvantage compared to foreign companies who routinely paid bribes. For example, in one discussion between executives of German and American companies operating in China, the German executive said, "We do not have to follow the same rules that you [the American company] do, so we will always win."

Accordingly, the United States commenced negotiations in the Organization of Economic Cooperation and Development (OECD) to obtain the agreement of trading partners to enact legislation similar to the FCPA. Ten years later, 34 countries signed the OECD Convention on Combating Bribery of Foreign Public Officials in International Business Transactions. Later, 43 countries signed the Anti-Corruption Convention, with Article 16 regarding bribing foreign government officials or public officials as a crime, with supporting jurisdiction, legal cooperation, and extradition provisions.

One example of the consequences of such agreements occurred in April 2004, when Lucent Technologies Inc. fired four executives at its Chinese operations, including the president, the chief operating officer, a marketing executive, and a finance manager, for violations of the FCPA, the company said in a filing with the U.S. SEC.[1] An analyst with an investment bank told *Caijing*:

> You have to get into the market to start businesses before everything is okay, and you have to adapt yourself to all kinds of "rules" . . . If the FCPA is strictly applied, 100 percent . . . have violated the law, whether they are American or European.

Lucent also said it uncovered problems in its operations in 23 foreign countries, including Brazil, India, Indonesia, the Philippines, and Russia, among others. What is interesting is that when reporting the story, Reuters quoted a risk-management expert as saying many multinational companies believe that corruption is "part of the culture and part of society" in China.

As discussed, culture evolves with history, mediated in the immediate by politics and the integration of new ideas. Although corruption often corrodes certain aspects of society as the result of social pressures, seldom does corruption become part of the widely accepted social culture. What does surface is a phenomenon that sociologists call social corruption. For example, in some countries, hospitals or physicians might prescribe unnecessary medicines to receive gratuities from pharmaceutical companies. In many countries, close relationships are obligatory to conducting business; however, there is a Chinese saying that a mare doesn't run on an empty stomach. This implies that, from the course of business, some benefit always results.

---

[1]News sources for this section: *China Daily*, November 9, 2004; *Caijing,* April 4, 2004; Wang Yichao, Zhang Fan, caijing.hexun.com/english/2004/040420/**lucent**.htm; "Lucent Fires Top Chinese Executives for Bribery," by Sumner Lemon, IDG News Services, April 7, 2004; *China Daily,* April 18, 2004

The aphorism "Everybody does it" does not hold up to scrutiny, and experience demonstrates that business can be conducted cleanly and honestly. In working with developing leaders, coaches have the opportunity to bring out the best in their clients.

Ethical Checklist

The concept of business ethics has come to generally mean determining what is right or wrong in the organization, and then doing what is right. This concept is fraught with difficulty; some assert there is always a right thing to do based on moral principle, and others believe the right action depends upon the situation. Often, to alleviate this basic dilemma, we convert what we consider ethical today into a law, regulation, or rule tomorrow.

Another way to approach minimizing the possibility of ethical dilemmas and resolving them in an ethical manner is to use an ethical checklist, such as this one:

1. *The legality or policy test*—Does my decision break the law or corporate policy?

2. *The "newspaper, light-of-day, or family" test*—Would I want to read about my decision in the local newspaper tomorrow morning? Would I want my family to know about what I decided?

3. *Respect all*—Have I encouraged people of other cultures to express themselves in their uniqueness, regardless of the prevailing corporate culture?

4. *Involvement test*—Have I involved others in the decision?

5. *Walk the talk; pursue authenticity*—Does the staff perceive me as motivational and able to retain highly capable people?

6. *Personal responsibility*—Do I accept personally the consequences of my actions?

7. *Relevant information*—Does the organization practice glass–wall management, in which people openly communicate their actions and objectives as they relate to organizational initiatives?

8. *Fairness test*—How do I interpret fairness?

Co-created Cultures

Although these evaluations may be of assistance in the initial stages when a person is integrating into a new culture, such tests might lead to one of many popular myths, such as the following:

- Ethics only restates the obvious, so just do the right thing.

- It is obvious that honesty is important, but if a company has continuing occasions of corruption, it should list honesty as a value in the company code of ethics.

- Codes of ethics should change with the needs of society and the organization.

- Our organization is not in trouble with the law; therefore, we are being ethical.

- Western science, economics, and politics are universal.

Given the multiplicity of cultures and the concomitant array of ways to view ethics, the challenge becomes how to find unanimity as people bridge cultures. One culture's value systems, morality, science, and politics are not universal; rather, they describe thought processes and behaviors particular to that culture. Even though one culture's mores or sciences may be embraced by another, this is not assurance that the transference is collective or universal in nature.

The goal of the coach in intercultural settings is to motivate individual behaviors and facilitate human interactions. A culturally aware coach can catalyze a neutral zone that bridges the gaps between the cultures, instead of forcing everyone to act in the same way. In addition, the coach can stimulate the client to:

- Explore ways to define the mutual space to involve others, such that all parties can contribute.

- Recognize and understand cultural diversity, personal accountability, and the power to change.

- Induce the formation of a third culture, or space in which people evolve new ways of accomplishing tasks.

- Constructively assess the behaviors of the other culture, and possibly transform those behaviors.

Co-creating cultures can happen on the business level as well as the personal level. For example, a company expands operations into East Asia (Japan, Korea, and China) and decides to use Asian social processes (relationships, expectations, harmony, and reciprocity) along with Western business processes (disciplined communication channels, responsibility and accountability, business ethics). On a personal level, some of the employees of this company will bring their home culture with them, or try to find it in the new host culture. Sometimes, this approach equates to a convoy mentality in which the persons enter the host culture together only with others sympathetic with the home culture. Other employees will enter this new culture immediately and encompass the host culture in its entirety. Still others will learn to balance host and home cultures by maintaining vestiges of their home culture that are supportive, and integrating those aspects of the host culture that feel comfortable.

The culturally aware coach chooses not to judge the process of the sojourner, but rather to motivate the client to search for new possibilities. For example, I (Charles) coached an American who had been living in Tokyo for two years. One particular evening as we left the office at the end of the session, my client seemed concerned that his wife had the car because he had never ridden the Tokyo subway. Here was an opportunity as coach to help this client see that riding the subway gave him the opportunity to venture out into places that driving would never have taken him.

In another instance, a young Indian couple was adjusting quite well to their new Melbourne home; however, during our conversations, the female partner remarked that she had been gaining weight just staying in the house all day. In India, women's routines of family life often are led from meal to meal, preparing and conversing with family and friends. Because she had no friends or family, she was totally engrossed in an unfamiliar world without the benefits of either culture. As a coach, one of my objectives was to stimulate actions in which she could both venture out into the Melbourne world and maintain the traditional value of a home-cooked Indian meal, ready when her husband returned from work.

Co-creating a culture with family members, colleagues, and friends is a strategy that allows freedom to balance those aspects of life that mean the most to the people who are moving into a new culture. The coach has a responsibility to encourage the development of strategies that lead not just to integrating within the community, but also to personal transformation.

Best Practices and Considerations for Coaching Ethically across Cultures

The world environment is in constant change, with countries re-creating themselves along cultural and ethnic borders, workforces increasing their diversity, competition intensifying trade relations, and technology outpacing yesterday's innovators and innovations. Within this mélange of disparate and often conflicting pressures, the individual searches for ways to lead colleagues, develop leadership in others, thrive during cultural transitions, and live a more balanced and rewarding life. In support of the coach's mandate to create strategies that meet these demands, we offer the following considerations within the framework of the International Coach Federation (ICF) *Coaching Competencies and Code of Ethics* (*http://www.coachfederation.org/eweb/*).

- We encourage you to not assume that commonalities exist between you and your clients, or between your clients and their partners or staff. Be self-aware, taking your beliefs into account in your approach to coaching clients. Be aware of your clients' culture and how that shapes their mind-set and practices, including their approach to coaching (what is appropriate, what is ethical, and what is not). Recognize that there might be many cultural groups within a country. China, for example, has more than 50 nationalities, nearly as many languages, and at least five major cuisines. This reality ties into the ICF's first two coaching competencies, which address meeting ethical guidelines and establishing the coaching agreement.

- Remember to evaluate and interpret situations from a multicultural frame of reference; for example, different approaches to time. For instance, the Latin cultures in which Marilyn has lived, and the Bahamas, where she has traveled, have a different sense of time than U.S. cultures. A client from another culture may say he will complete his fieldwork, action plan, or goal by a certain date, and then does not. A culturally aware coach will check to see whether this missed deadline has to do with the client's cultural orientation to time, or whether something else is getting in the way. If a client from another culture runs late for appointments, a review of the coaching policy is appropriate, or the coach can explore cultural differences with the client, and they can implement a mutual plan to meet the needs of each person. The choice gets back to who does the adjusting, when, and how much, which is a common thread in intercultural work.

◆ Ethical considerations in the multicultural coaching agreement include confidentiality. How far will you take confidentiality if a client discloses illegal, or what you would consider unethical, behavior? Will you specify confidentiality limits in a written agreement at the beginning of coaching, or wait and see whether the issue comes up? If you are working within an organization, would you have to report this situation to someone in the organization? To the legal authorities? Note: "Know the law" can be very challenging when laws vary from state to state, as well as from country to country.

◆ Know the difference and importance of *high-context culture* and *low-context culture*. For example, in a high-context culture (such as Asia, Latin America, Southern Europe), nonverbal, indirect communication is important, with the physical context relied upon for information; whereas, in a low-context culture (such as the United States, United Kingdom, and Northern and Central Europe), the communication is direct and less dependent on nonverbal cues and the environment. How will this difference affect how you formulate your coaching agreement? Will you meet in person, on the phone, or by email? How much do you put in writing, and how much should be verbal agreement?

◆ Gaining clarity regarding the distinctions between counseling, coaching, and consulting may be more challenging interculturally. Also, making a referral for counseling in a culture where saving face is important might be very tricky. How would you let the client know about additional resources without labeling the client as emotionally unhealthy?

◆ Establishing trust and intimacy (ICF coaching competency number 3) will be established over time across cultural boundaries by demonstrating respect for the client's beliefs and values (both individual and cultural). This process may take less or more time than in your native culture. It is not that trust is hard to build; it is more about how trust is perceived. To Westerners, trust is often perceived as being developed through a series of transactions during which the other person performs to defined standards. In other words, behavior leads to relationship. In many Asian cultures, a level of trust must be established before people respond appropriately; in other words, the relationship defines the behavior. To develop trust, the coach needs to understand the perception of trust that the client has incorporated into her relationship-building schema. Intellectual property, an ethical consideration, is also viewed differently in a collective versus an individualistic culture. In a collective culture, intellectual property might be seen as belonging to everyone rather than to an individual. If you are a member of an individualistic culture, and you find someone else is using your material without recognition or attribution, what do you do?

◆ Related to coaching presence, listening with intuition can transcend cultures. "Presence means bringing your self when you coach—your values, passion, creativity, emotion and discerning judgment—to any given moment with the client" (O'Neill, 2000). The intercultural coach effectively demonstrates curiosity, seeking to learn about other cultures, just as coaches, in discovery, seek to learn about clients. Tolerance of ambiguity and flexibility are key multicultural, as well as executive coaching, competencies. Realize that accepting cultural differences does not mean agreement, but, rather, not judging. Recognizing there are differences is the first step out of ethnocentrism, which, like level one listening (co-active coaching), filters everything through one's own lens or that of one's culture. More specifically, we hear the words of the other person, but the focus is on what it means to us.

While actively listening, the intercultural coach will attend to clients' values and beliefs and how those things affect the clients' ethical behavior. The coach might also address these issues while asking coaching questions. Examples of questions that relate to intercultural coaching include: "Will this action move you closer to honoring your individual or cultural values?" "If you make this decision, what values (individual, cultural) will you have honored?"

With direct communication, both creating awareness and planning and goal setting considerations include how direct or how polite to be, which may include how much, as a coach, to challenge perspectives and confront clients when they have not followed through with their committed action plan.

Understanding cultural perceptions, discerning trust-building processes, and expressing cultural curiosity are some of the strategies important in building intercultural competency. These strategies also apply specifically, however, to interactions between the coach and people of different cultural and ethical values.

◆ Humility, including not being afraid to not know, being willing to ask questions, and seeking understanding, is another aspect of intercultural coaching presence. Coaches should be aware, though, that in some cultures, those with status are expected to have the answers. This caution pertains to being respectful of the hierarchy of the culture. Some cultures have clear teacher/student roles rather than partnerships, and the coach and client will refer to each other by title and last name rather than by first names. (Do not assume!) Who is considered the expert, the client or the coach? Some Asians do not believe it is appropriate to ask questions of a person in authority. Who the expert is, and how she should be approached, vary from one culture to the next. For example, an American once told me (Marilyn) that he was corrected for calling a German by his first name at a business meeting. In Europe, coaches' credentials and degrees may have more to do with being selected than in the United States. Be aware of how your status, gender, role, power, and culture are viewed by your multicultural clients.

Bridging Cultures: Case Studies in Ethics

There are three basic ways to view a person bridging cultures:

- A person moving into a new culture (inward looking)
- A person looking outward toward global business or the world in general (outward looking)
- A person working inside (looking within) a homogeneous culture

There probably is no such environment of complete homogeneity because physical or cultural diversities exist in even seemingly uniform cultures. For example, in China, people from Sichuan, Beijing, Shanghai, and Hong Kong all have distinct languages, cultures, and behaviors.

When coaching executives who move across borders, one issue that repeatedly arises is how to respond to the culture of people that one meets. For example, one day as I (Charles) sat in a Shanghai office of a divisional VP of a large global company, I noticed that during the course of the day the executive, a native of India, received three telephone calls.

The first call was from an American. During this call, the executive reclined in his seat, put his feet upon the desk, and talked about baseball and the kids. His accent was almost a drawl, even though he was a highly educated Indian national, who spoke Queen's English. Next, a call came from a Japanese colleague, to which the VP responded in a very upright position, feet on the floor, and using a soft, almost humble voice. In a following call from a Chinese employee, the executive leaned into more of an aggressive position, speaking rapid-fire, although friendly and courteous. My observation has been that quite often Indians are very observant and respond to people in ways appropriate to the other culture.

In another coaching session with a Swedish executive, I described this scenario, and his reaction was astonishment. He asked, "Why should I change myself to meet the culture of another? I am no chameleon!"

The ethical dilemma posed is how to match styles to improve communication, yet not sacrifice one's own morals, culture, and ethics. Quite often, in crossing borders, we hear, "This is the way we do it here." In some situations, such as matching styles for effective communication, some people would argue the necessity of conformance; others would remain solidly in their own paradigm. In other situations, such as when one is giving a payment or favor to elicit a sympathetic response, many other factors influence the decision process.

When one considers bribery, for example, as an unwarranted payment to elicit behavior or a favor that otherwise would not be

239

bestowed, there are both macro and micro effects. Bribery is also a case of governance. The first macro effect is the law. As we have seen, most countries sponsor laws concerning the illegality of payments used to educe inappropriate benefits; for example, the United States has the Foreign Corrupt Practices Act (FCPA), mentioned earlier in the chapter, to which most American companies espouse compliance and concomitant zero-tolerance for infractions. Quite often, these laws are not enforced consistently at foreign subsidiary levels; however, nor are they enforced strictly by government organizations.

Illicit payments, besides breaking the law, lead to inertias in procurement and sales processes by fostering a need to negotiate outside normal business parameters. The transaction expenses add to overall product costs and the subsequent premium to the consumer.

A more insidious cost is the effect on morale within the organization. My (Charles) experience from working in organizations that tolerate even a modicum of corruption has shown me that teamwork starts to break down. When one person of a particular level of capability, and resulting responsibility and comparable reward, looks across at a colleague, what is observed is often the corresponding balance in capability and reward. If other colleagues have the same perceived capability, but with inappropriate levels of reward, such as that catalyzed by illicit payments, people naturally respond in less than cooperative ways.

Culture greatly affects this level of discontent. In the United States, India, and Japan, imbalances in capability and responsibility are likely tolerated to similar extents, but for much different reasons. In India, cultural influences of such religious beliefs as *karma* and cultural tolerance may allow a sense of "no expectations, no disappointments." The United States has an environment of relatively high levels of job mobility. Individuals are generally aware that inequalities may exist during organizational change, and that these imbalances are usually transitory. These two aspects of organizations lead to a belief that "fairness" will eventually win. In addition, in the United States, the cultural tendencies of individualism and performance often drive discontent and departure from the organization. In Japan, intricate systems of relationship and obligation constrain behavior that runs counter to the prevailing sense of harmony.

In China, there are perhaps unexpected outcomes. Whereas in decidedly hierarchical organizations, persons in power rule without much employee discontent, with relationship more critical than performance, in emerging models of Chinese companies, merit-based reward systems play a major role in the creation of human-resource policies. A commonality in both forms of organizations is that people will often respond by creating an environment of doing what one is expected to do. This kind of organizational culture often leads to employees experiencing palpable apathy and passing responsibility upward.

When coaching a South African executive moving to Japan, he mentioned to me (Charles) that he was having difficulties in reaching out to the Japanese. As we explored the reasons for his discomfort, he said that, as an Orthodox Jew, he was allowed to bow to the Japanese priest only once a year, thus causing him to be hampered in his attempts to show respect. The question then arises: "Should one forsake one's own morals to avoid cultural chauvinism?" In this case, we explored using such other outward behaviors as fluency in Japanese greetings to demonstrate his awareness of Japanese culture. This led to other interactions at work as he learned appropriate behaviors from Japanese colleagues directly.

When coaching people in intercultural settings, one should be aware of how cultural differences affect relationships and performance. Neither the coach nor the client may be aware of the specific cultural factors that are governing results; therefore, the coach has to ask questions that draw out possible client inertias to effective ethical frameworks and behaviors. An example would be to explore the level of responsibility that a person takes in intercultural communication. In answers to such queries, intercultural coaches often hear such comments as, "They do not understand me," "They do not listen very well," or "They never speak in meetings."

One approach to helping clients transcend cultural barriers is to motivate them to seek out the cultural or organizational reasons for the seeming lack of understanding or response. Another approach is to explore the clients' own capabilities to assume responsibility for suboptimal communication.

Conclusion

This chapter examines how ethical variances among cultures affect the process of coaching people of different cultures. The framework was set by looking at what culture is, and how cultural values drive ethics, noting the distinction between cultural and individual values in coaching. We have identified awareness as a primary competency in intercultural coaching, including both creating awareness in the client and an awareness of the client and coach's cultural values and ethics. Action is a necessary adjunct to awareness, and we explored who will do how much adjusting when it comes to intercultural variances, including ethics.

Considerations in the intercultural coaching process include cultural variations in building trust and establishing credibility; indirect v. direct and formal v. informal communication; confidentiality; the importance of presence; and evaluation of situations from an intercultural perspective. Awareness leads to knowledge and, when applied in practice, develops competencies. Coaches may also serve in co-creating a neutral third culture or space that bridges cultural gaps, a place where diversity can be leveraged and celebrated, and each person's contribution recognized.

Intercultural coaching ethics, especially when coaching with organizations, also is affected by legal and governance issues. Governance, or the process by which an organization or society conducts its behavior, is one spoke of the rudder, with leadership and transparency comprising the other two spokes, that guide organizations through ethical decision-making processes. Here, the coach's role in developing leaders and teams in intercultural organizations is to support the same intercultural competencies required of the coach (flexibility, global mind-set, nonjudgmental approach, curiosity).

The cases and discussion presented again demonstrate the key question of who does the adjusting, and how much, in relation to intercultural values and ethics. The intercultural coach can help individuals maintain integrity—clarity about ethics and how to apply them in the multicultural environment.

The role of the intercultural coach as an agent of integration and transformation is supported by the competencies of flexibility, curiosity, humility, and global mind-set. Awareness is identified as a primary competency in intercultural coaching, including not only creating awareness in the client, but also an awareness of the client and coach's cultural values and ethics. This awareness can prevent ethical dilemmas and transgressions.

REFERENCES

O'Neill, M.B. (2000). *Executive coaching with backbone and heart.* San Francisco: Jossey Bass.

Said, E.W. (2002). *Culture and resistance.* Cambridge, MA: South End Press.

10

Coaching to Come

Patrick Williams, William H. Lindberg, and Sharon K. Anderson

The Future of Coaching by Patrick Williams

There's no turning back. People today desire to live life on purpose, and need vital, results-oriented connections despite the rapidly increasing pace of change, and a lack of sustainable relationships. Coaching will permeate society in the coming years, and become available to everyone. We will see coaches in every organization and group, from the family unit to the largest conglomerates on the planet. Coaching is on its way to becoming bigger and more successful than any other form of organizational investment in the future. Workplace coaching will serve to ensure employee retention, team cohesiveness, sales and production increases, and overall employee effectiveness and satisfaction. The field of life coaching, or personal coaching, embodies those areas of coaching that are about the whole person; these areas might include health and wellness, life purpose, relationships, and work satisfaction. The conversations in life coaching have a larger landscape and scope-of-life design; personal or life coaching is available for relationships, parenting, wellness and health issues, spiritual development, and retirement, just to name a few.

> *"Executives and HR managers know coaching is the most potent tool for inducing positive personal change, ensuring better-than-average odds of success, and making the change stick for the long term."*
>
> —IVY BUSINESS JOURNAL

The coaching profession is experiencing dynamic growth and change. It will continue to interact developmentally with social, economic, corporate, and political processes; to draw on the knowledge base of diverse disciplines; to enhance its intellectual and professional maturity; and to establish itself as the most powerful and effective tool for success in any area. As a note of caution, life and personal coaches must be extra careful to not be perceived as psychotherapists or mental-health counselors. Coaching does not focus on any type of treatment of mental illness or severe emotional difficulties. However, as long as the relationship follows the professional guidelines and competencies involved in coaching, human emotions and overcoming mental blocks may be part of the conversations. All coaches should be trained to refer to mental-health professionals when appropriate, and to have a licensed mental-health professional available to them for consulting when necessary.

We have attempted to give a history of the coaching profession and its desire to be a publicly recognized and understood service with high standards. Yet, as we know, there will always be charlatans and unethical people who call themselves coaches and do not exhibit the desirable standard of practice. Most professions face that dilemma as they grow and develop. Our hope is that, both through professional practice and increasing public awareness, the coaching profession will be distinguished in the public eye from poorly trained or unprofessional self-proclaimed coaches.

Thoughts on the Future of Coaching and Coach Training by William H. Lindberg

In exploring the future of coaching and coach training, it is worthwhile to consider the exponential growth and heightened awareness of the field in the recent past. The International Coach Federation will have held its Tenth Annual professional meeting in 2005. There are currently 7,500 members and 129 chapters operating in 32 countries.[1] This represents a dramatic increase in the number of coaches that were members of ICF five years earlier. At the time of this writing, there are 29 coach training programs in North America, Europe, Asia, and Australia currently accredited by the ICF, with many more in the queue applying for accreditation. Interest in the field of coaching has catapulted the profession forward during the past decade, as evidenced by the wide array of articles in the business and popular press.

Among the mitigating forces to this growth, however, have been the difficulties many prospective and active coaches have experienced in undertaking coaching as a full-time enterprise. Economic viability has proved elusive for many entrepreneurial coaches. Frequently, coaching is conducted as a part of a portfolio of offerings such as training or consulting. There can also be confusion in the marketplace as to specifically what qualifies as coaching as opposed to other

---

[1] *Proceedings of the Second ICF Coaching Research Symposium*, I.F. Stein, F. Campone, & L.J. Page (Eds.)(p. vi). This is a publication of the International Coach Federation, Washington, D.C., 2005.

activities. As the future unfolds, it will be interesting to see whether the growing awareness and demand for coaching will expand to accommodate the legions of newly minted coaches entering the marketplace.

On the coach training front, there have been numerous independent, free-standing coach training programs offering courses for the past 15 years. More recently, university-based programs at institutions such as Georgetown, New York University, Royal Roads (Canada), and a prospective program at the University of Texas—Dallas are emerging. The professional organization for coach training programs is ACTO (the Association of Coach Training Organizations, see *www.acto1.com* for further information).

Among the current initiatives being undertaken by ACTO, in collaboration with the ICF, are the promotion and establishment of credentials and accreditation standards. Likewise, the enhancement of evidence-based, empirical research is gaining momentum. This research will hopefully validate and support the claims and experience that coaching is, in fact, valuable for executives, organizations, and individuals. Pursuing this research holds the promise of adding a critical dimension and deeper evidence to the discussion surrounding the efficacy of coaching.

Coaching and Wellness by Sharon K. Anderson

As a professor in a counseling program it seems somewhat serendipitous that over the last two years we have had master and doctoral students request training in wellness from a coaching philosophy. For these students the concept of wellness is broad and encompasses all parts of a person's life: the personal, including emotions and cognitions; relationships at home, work, and play; the work/career journey, the spiritual and meaning of life focus; and the physical, taking care of the mind and body. A future wellness and coaching model seems reasonable at both the masters and doctoral levels. This likely calls for disciplines in higher education (i.e., counseling, psychology, education, human development, exercise and sport science, health and nutrition, social psychology) to come together to develop an interdisciplinary program that not only trains masters and doctoral students in knowledge and skill but also suggests the opportunity for research and outcome-based studies.

With such an endeavor there are a host of positive outcomes. The field of coaching gains from another experience or level of training and research. The prospective students of the program receive training that views people as having many pieces in life that impact and interface with each other. The client gains from working with professionals that view and work with their clients as a whole being.

The Emergence of Academic Degrees in Personal and Professional Coaching: What Does This Mean to the Future of Coaching? by Patrick Williams

In my book, *Therapist as Life Coach: Transforming Your Practice in 2002* (Norton Books), I predicted that with the evolution of the coaching profession and the proliferation of coach training organizations, the next logical step would be graduate degrees in coaching. Just two or three colleges in the last half of the 20th century and the beginning of the 21st century offered such certificates or degrees. George Washington University became the first ICF-accredited coach training program after starting as a certificate program within the Organizational Development department. The University of Sydney (Australia), spearheaded by Dr. Anthony Grant, offered the first MA in Coaching Psychology in the late 1990s. Those two were soon followed by other colleges offering graduate classes in coaching, some leading to certificates in coaching as part of a graduate degree in a related field, such as organizational development, management, or leadership.

As of 2005, more than two dozen colleges and universities offer either a certificate program or a full graduate degree in coaching. The valuable addition of academic institutions to the growth of the coaching profession is very welcome. This trend adds courses of study that underpin the actual coaching relationship, including personality development, developmental psychology, theories of human change, research methodology, organizational development, and cross-cultural issues.

This proliferation of academic programs in coaching also parallels the path of the field of clinical psychology. In 1949, the historical Colorado event called the Boulder Conference was held to create the field of clinical psychology and PhD programs that would teach the science-practitioner model of academic studies. This model focused on both practical application of skills and the scientific rigor and knowledge of evidence-based research and research methodologies. A later conference in 1973 in Vail, Colorado, (hence called the Vail Conference) offered an alternative for the learner who did not want to be a researcher but who sought the specific applied skills to be a masterful psychologist. This model, which became known as the scholar-professional model, created the momentum for the Psy.D, or Doctor of Psychology. Today, more students are enrolled in Psy.D programs, even though more PhD programs exist by number.

Many of the graduate-level coaching certificates are offered by very recognizable institutions, such as Georgetown University, University of Texas, JFK University, Duke University, New York University, Villanova University, George Mason University, Fielding University, and othersóall accredited and long-established institutions of higher learning. Georgetown University and Royal Roads

University (Canada) are Accredited Coach Training Programs and many others (such as George Mason University and Fielding International University) are aligning their programs with ICF standards and competencies.

Other institutions, such as Walden University and International University of Professional Studies, allow ìalternative educationî and creative degree design with an emphasis on self-directed learning with a mentor and distance-learning modalities coupled with classroom learning by the learner's choice and committee approval. Colorado State University has started conversations with me to create a PhD in Interdisciplinary Studies and Health and Wellness Coaching.

Most of the graduate institutions are focused on executive or corporate applications, but a few (such as IUPS.edu) are focused on a more general education in coaching and human development that can be applied across the client spectrum. And several in the United Kingdom are offering degrees or certificates in professional coaching (University of Wolverhamptom, Middlesex University, Oxford Brookes, and others).

I interviewed representatives from four different and unique institutions and asked them all the same questions (University of Sydney, Fielding University, Georgetown University, and International University of Professional Studies):

1. Why offer a graduate degree/certificate in coaching?

2. Are you particularly interested in ICF guidelines for coaching certification?

3. What do you think the future of degrees in coaching is in relation to established coach training schools?

4. What is unique about your program?

5. How will your students impact research in coaching?

There is not space here to include all of their thoughtful and enlightening responses, but I can say that each of them saw its interest in being on the cutting edge of an evolving profession and assisting in creating or affirming an academic philosophy of coaching and evidenced-based research on the skill sets of coaching and the predictable outcomes for coaches and clients. In other words, documenting what really works and why.

All of the four representatives I spoke with stated that graduate education in coaching adds to the credibility of the profession and may also assist in the future of self-regulation as the various governments look highly on graduate degrees.

Anthony Grant from University of Sydney states: "This trend will encourage private coaching schools to raise the bar, and I'm sure we all agree that this is good for the students, good for the coaching industry, and good for the schools."

Dr. Leni Wildflower of Fielding University says, "There is room for both and a need for both academic programs and coach training organizations. For those who want grounding in a long-term academically rigorous program, the degree programs are the answer. For those who just want the skill training and may use the coach approach as part of their job, or they want to be an entrepreneurial private coach, high-quality coach training may be the answer for them as well."

Chris Wall, MA, MCC, of Georgetown University's coaching program states: "We have found over the past few years that the corporate consumers are more and more educated and savvy about coaching, and, in many cases, are requiring that coaches they hire be ICF certified. I am totally interested in raising the standards of coaching, including incorporating the newest thinking about coaching that is based on developmental theory, including cognitive capacity, and linking ways to align coaching moves with the evidence that is developmentally available. This will only serve to strengthen the power of coaching in the world."

And Dr. Irv Katz, chancellor of the innovative International University for Professional Studies states that: "Research in coaching is essential if the field is to gain the credibility it deserves. Step by step, gains through coaching must be documented. The leadership in the field of coaching recognizes this. And if coaches are going to do the research or be a part of the research being done, IUPS stands ready to assist those researchers in earning their doctorates."

Steve Mitten, MCC and ICF president 2005 says, "Coaching is a young and evolving profession. Itís too early to predict the many ways future coaching professionals will learn their skills and provide value to their clients. However, in terms of increased credibility, greater effectiveness, and a better overall understanding of what is at the heart of what we are already intuitively doing with our clients, the growing partnership between researchers, academia, and the coaching profession is a win for everyone."

So as you can see, the profession of coaching is growing in tandem with the academic theory, rigor, research, and application that comes with graduate education. As the profession of coaching continues to spread globally, the impact of institutions of higher learning offering graduate certificates and degrees in coaching will be a trend to watch in the next few years.

Will this mean that in the near future you must have a graduate degree to be a coach? Probably not. But graduate education expands the knowledge base, challenges the status quo, and will raise the bar for training programs. And similarly, the standards of best practice as taught by the International Coach Federation and other coaching organizations will hopefully be endorsed and absorbed into the curriculums of the colleges. For our profession to be self-regulated and publicly recognized, it must have the partnership of academia and the coaching profession at large. This partnership and growth of our profession through research, applied theory, and quality skill acquisition bodes well for all of us interested in our profession thriving not just surviving.

Appendix A

The ICF CODE OF ETHICS

Part One: The ICF Philosophy of Coaching

The International Coach Federation adheres to a form of coaching that honors the client as the expert in his/her life and work and believes that every client is creative, resourceful, and whole. Standing on this foundation, the coach's responsibility is to:

- Discover, clarify, and align with what the client wants to achieve
- Encourage client self-discovery
- Elicit client-generated solutions and strategies
- Hold the client responsible and accountable

Part Two: The ICF Definition of Coaching

Professional coaching is an ongoing professional relationship that helps people produce extraordinary results in their lives, careers, businesses, or organizations. Through the process of coaching, clients deepen their learning, improve their performance, and enhance their quality of life.

In each meeting, the client chooses the focus of conversation, while the coach listens and contributes observations and questions. This interaction creates clarity and moves the client into action. Coaching accelerates the client's progress by providing greater focus and awareness of choice. Coaching concentrates on where clients are now and what they are willing to do to get where they want to be in the future. ICF member coaches and ICF credentialed coaches recognize that results are a matter of the client's intentions, choices, and actions, supported by the coach's efforts and application of the coaching process.

Part Three: The ICF Standards of Ethical Conduct

Professional Conduct At Large

As a coach:

1. I will conduct myself in a manner that reflects positively upon the coaching profession and I will refrain from engaging in conduct or making statements that may negatively impact the public's understanding or acceptance of coaching as a profession.

2. I will not knowingly make any public statements that are untrue or misleading, or make false claims in any written documents relating to the coaching profession.

3. I will respect different approaches to coaching. I will honor the efforts and contributions of others and not misrepresent them as my own.

4. I will be aware of any issues that may potentially lead to the misuse of my influence by recognizing the nature of coaching and the way in which it may affect the lives of others.

5. I will at all times strive to recognize personal issues that may impair, conflict, or interfere with my coaching performance or my professional relationships. Whenever the facts and circumstances necessitate, I will promptly seek professional assistance and determine the action to be taken, including whether it is appropriate to suspend or terminate my coaching relationship(s).

6. As a trainer or supervisor of current and potential coaches, I will conduct myself in accordance with the ICF Code of Ethics in all training and supervisory situations.

7. I will conduct and report research with competence, honesty, and within recognized scientific standards. My research will be carried out with the necessary approval or consent from those involved, and with an approach that will reasonably protect participants from any potential harm. All research efforts will be performed in a manner that complies with the laws of the country in which the research is conducted.

8. I will accurately create, maintain, store, and dispose of any records of work done in relation to the practice of coaching in a way that promotes confidentiality and complies with any applicable laws.

9. I will use ICF member contact information (email addresses, telephone numbers, etc.) only in the manner and to the extent authorized by the ICF.

Professional Conduct with Clients

10. I will be responsible for setting clear, appropriate, and culturally sensitive boundaries that govern any physical contact that I may have with my clients.

11. I will not become sexually involved with any of my clients.

12. I will construct clear agreements with my clients, and will honor all agreements made in the context of professional coaching relationships.

13. I will ensure that, prior to or at the initial session, my coaching client understands the nature of coaching, the bounds of confidentiality, financial arrangements, and other terms of the coaching agreement.

14. I will accurately identify my qualifications, expertise, and experience as a coach.

15. I will not intentionally mislead or make false claims about what my client will receive from the coaching process or from me as a coach.

16. I will not give my clients or prospective clients information or advice I know or believe to be misleading.

17. I will not knowingly exploit any aspect of the coach–client relationship for my personal, professional, or monetary advantage or benefit.

18. I will respect the client's right to terminate coaching at any point during the process. I will be alert to indications that the client is no longer benefiting from our coaching relationship.

19. If I believe the client would be better served by another coach, or by another resource, I will encourage the client to make a change.

20. I will suggest that my clients seek the services of other professionals when deemed appropriate or necessary.

21. I will take all reasonable steps to notify the appropriate authorities in the event a client discloses an intention to endanger self or others.

Confidentiality/Privacy

22. I will respect the confidentiality of my client's information, except as otherwise authorized by my client, or as required by law.

23. I will obtain agreement from my clients before releasing their names as clients or references, or any other client-identifying information.

24. I will obtain agreement from the person being coached before releasing information to another person compensating me.

Conflicts of Interest

25. I will seek to avoid conflicts between my interests and the interests of my clients.

26. Whenever any actual conflict of interest or the potential for a conflict of interest arises, I will openly disclose it and fully discuss with my client how to deal with it in whatever way best serves my client.

27. I will disclose to my client all anticipated compensation from third parties that I may receive for referrals of that client.

28. I will only barter for services, goods, or other non-monetary remuneration when it will not impair the coaching relationship.

Part Four: The ICF Pledge of Ethics

As a professional coach, I acknowledge and agree to honor my ethical obligations to my coaching clients and colleagues and to the public at large. I pledge to comply with the ICF Code of Ethics, to treat people with dignity as independent and equal human beings, and to model these standards with those whom I coach. If I breach this Pledge of Ethics or any part of the ICF Code of Ethics, I agree that the ICF in its sole discretion may hold me accountable for so doing. I further agree that my accountability to the ICF for any breach may include loss of my ICF membership and/or my ICF credentials.

Appendix B

Professional Coaching Language for Greater Public Understanding

David Matthew Prior, MCC, MBA
Co-chair, ICF Ethics & Standards Committee

INTRODUCTION

The Profession of Coaching Is Not Clearly Understood by the Public

Despite an estimated 20 years of business existence and practice, the profession of coaching clearly remains in its infancy. Although many people in the United States are beginning to hear about personal and business coaches, the vast majority of the public is still unknowledgeable about what a coach actually *does*. More often than not, coaching is (incorrectly) understood by an unknowing public to be a *virtual version* of modern therapy; this misperception and comparison may be attributed to the public's face-value recognition that regular, ongoing meetings with a coach look like therapy sessions.

The Evolution of Business Coaching

Coaching has been conducted in the business world for a long time, as consultants have worked with CEOs, executives, and their business teams. Utilizing and combining the processes of business coaching and consulting, and strategic and action planning activities often naturally address individual behaviors, motivation, and related personal improvement. As a result of its evolutionary process, coaching has expanded from the business environment to the 'life" environment where similar action-oriented work with the coach addresses matters outside the work environment.

Personal and Life Coaching

The natural outgrowth and extension of this business-related work is known as personal or life coaching, which includes a more encompassing focus on an individual's life as it relates to goal setting, outcome creation, and personal change management. It is perhaps from this broader focus that confusion arises for those who are unfamiliar with coaching. In the public's earnest effort to get a handle on what a coach does, misleading comparisons are quickly drawn to the therapeutic process, mainly because of the following personal service similarities:

- *Service delivery method*—regular face-to-face or telephone meetings
- *Content*—work and life challenges that an individual faces that often require change initiative and management
- *Activities performed by the professional coach*—interactive dialogue, intuitive listening, sounding-board feedback, client acknowledgment, etc.

268

Therefore, in order for knowledge to reach and benefit the end consumer, it is critical that increased efforts be made to distinguish, clarify, and honor the two professions so that the consumer can choose the most effective and appropriate service as dictated by individual life circumstances.

The ICF: Holding the Vision for a Self-Regulating Profession

The International Coach Federation (ICF) is the professional association of personal and business coaches that seeks to preserve the integrity of coaching around the globe. In order for the profession of coaching to continue to grow and dynamically create itself so that it can best serve all coaches and their clients, the ICF believes that coaching needs to remain a self-regulated profession.

To that end, it is *vital* that coaches learn to communicate to their prospects, their clients, the public, and the media in a language that does not confuse our profession with other seemingly like professions.

A NEW WAY OF LANGUAGING OUR PROFESSION: Observations and Suggestions for Coaches

The ICF regulatory committee has requested that I begin the process of investigating our use of coaching language as it relates to the mental health profession. I have listed my initial observations and suggestions. By no means is this document meant to be definitive, nor is the intent to rob anything from the wonderful process of coaching. The goal is to examine how we communicate what we do so that we differentiate and distinguish ourselves in the most powerful self-regulating frame.

1. Identify and reclassify coaching as a new profession

Don't call coaching: A helping profession

Do call coaching: A new profession

A personal development profession

A professional development profession

A personal growth profession

A self-improvement profession

2. Declare that coaching is not therapy

Many coaches spend a great portion of their introduction time talking to and educating the public as to the differences between coaching and therapy. This runs several risks:

* We confuse the public more.
* We focus our discussion on a dissertation of therapy and coaching principles.
* We defend coaching.
* We collapse the two professions.
* We try to justify why some people see both professionals at the same time.
* We make therapy wrong and coaching right.
* We enter discussions of defending why we are not licensed.

When a person tells you that coaching sounds like therapy, you can clarify and gently redirect *your* discussion to let them know it is not therapy, and that it is a *new profession* based in personal growth and client-initiated change. (See #1 in the previous section for other ways to language the profession.)

3. Speak about coaching results as non-feeling-based results

Many of our clients experience a greater sense of well-being after being coached and often *feel better* after a coaching call.

As great as that is, that is not our primary intent as coaches. Our work is focused on the ability and willingness of our clients to move forward and take action. The results of personal/life coaching are frequently likened to typical outcomes of therapy. Avoid making promises that imply *resultant feeling/emotional states or potential outcomes from improved mental health,* such as:

* A more fulfilled life
* A happier life
* A wonderful life
* A perfect life
* A healed life
* Healthier and happier relationships★

★ A distinction should be drawn between relationship counseling and relationship coaching. Generally speaking, relationship counseling is a therapeutic process that is oriented toward and focuses on the healing of pain, dysfunction, and conflict within a relationship. Relationship counseling is performed by licensed counselors. Relationship coaching focuses on identifying and clarifying the current goals of a relationship with an emphasis on action, accountability, and follow-through.

4. **Speak about your coaching business in business terms of your business/clients/clientele–not your coaching practice**

   Medical and mental health professionals often refer to their client base as their *practice.* While that is true of consultants as well, the term *consulting* is perceived as more of a business-oriented activity. When you talk about your work and the people who pay you, talk about your coaching *business,* coaching *clients*, and your coaching *clientele*. This will help alleviate the confusion between the *practitioners* of physical and mental health services—many of whom are required to be licensed by state regulatory agencies.

5. **Use a welcome packet instead of an intake packet**
   When beginning your work with a client, use language that speaks to the *first meeting, first call,* or *initial appointment.* If you send them a starting package of materials, call it a *welcome packet.* Intake and intake sessions are often processes associated with the mental health and social service fields.

6. **Emphasize *client-initiated* action and accountability**
   Coaching is unique in the manner in which the client interacts with the professional; the client is the driver in this professional relationship. It is the client who makes the final decision on and initiates the appropriate action. It is the client who agrees to abide by a system of accountability with the goal of being self-responsible and true to one's word. The coach fulfills the role of a facilitator in this process so that the client is fully empowered.

7. **Talk about what you do and how you do it, while using terms associated with professional coaching language instead of psychotherapy language**
   Obviously, an individual profession cannot claim ownership of language. It is helpful and useful for coaches to know the differences between what language is generally used in the realm of therapy as well as in coaching. Therefore, I have listed words that are associated in the general domain of each profession. The following lists are certainly not exhaustive. They are intended to educate the public by distinguishing the respective expertise of both professions.

Psychotherapy Language

Verbs

Unearth

Surface

Alleviate

Expose

Intervene

Adjust

Help/rescue

Heal (discomfort/pain)

Confront

Diagnose

Treat

Process (feelings)

Induce

Manifest (symptoms)

Content

Issues

Attitudes

Pain

Dysfunction

Symptoms and sources

Conditions

Disorder

Normal/abnormal

Unconscious/subconscious

Low self-worth

Mood disorders

Anxiety disorders

Social disorders

Suicide

Phobia

Addiction

Depression

Latent desires

Abusive behavior

Destructive behavior

Recurrent/repetitive patterns

Psychic roots of problems

Delusion

Types and subtypes of disorders

Severity levels

Transference

Adult/child behavior

Personality disorders

Antisocial behavior

Chronic behavior

Onset

Pathology

Dependence issues

Withdrawal

Loneliness and isolation (effects of)

Grief (effects and processing of)

Disturbance

Functioning level

Periods of

Panic attacks

Obsessive behavior

Functioning level

Impairment

Causation

Episodes

Trauma

Course (of a disorder)

Illness

Associated features (of a disorder or disease)

Clinical

Coaching Language

Verbs

Focus

Prioritize

Clarify

Measure

Move forward

Plan

Be proactive

Take action

Achieve

Delegate

Solve

Acknowledge

Brainstorm

Mind map

Request

Sort

Emphasize

Develop

Learn

Educate

Accomplish

Target

Complete

Take action

Train

Follow-up/Follow-through

Respond

Communicate

Content

Outcome

Positive action steps

Accountability

Self-improvement

Results

Self-responsibility

Projects

Measurement

Problems

Skills development

Money management

Systems

Organization

Management

Interpersonal communication skills

Intention

Purpose

Success

Balance

Choice

Options

Leadership

Actions

Tasks

Checklists

Possibilities

Response

Integrity

Deadline

Inquiry

Assignments

Follow-up and Follow-through

Goal setting

Vision and mission

Prompted self-discovery

Values

Planning

Strategies

Spiritual development/fulfillment (as a result of actions taken)

Please direct your comments, questions, and follow-up to:

David Matthew Prior, MCC, MBA

Co-chair, ICF Ethics & Standards Committee

Email: *david@getacoach.com*

Office: 201–825–2082 (EST)

Index